To Chin ... with love (handwritten)

ELEPHANTS AND MILLIPEDES

The organic revolution in Zambia
by
MERFYN TEMPLE

Merfyn Temple (signature)

**Dedicated to Ennias Michello
and all Zambia's organic growers and farmers**

ELEPHANTS AND MILLIPEDES

The organic revolution in Zambia

ISBN 0 9530369 0 1

Printed and produced by:
TWM Publishing
1 Horseshoe Park
Pangbourne
Berkshire
RG8 7JW
Tel: 0118 984 4337
Fax: 0118 984 4339

Published and distributed by:
Millipede Books
40 Thames Avenue
Pangbourne
Berkshire
RG8 7BY
Tel: 0118 984 5304

Typing & Preparation by Marian Merchant & Andy Kelley
Editing by Audrey Temple
Maps by Jane Clitheroe
Cover design by Robert Booth

Contents

THE COMPOST MAKERS

Zambia you are a land of forests
A land of sweeping savannas.
Zambia you are the home of a multitude of animals.
Mighty elephants live here and tiny millipedes.
Animals as powerful as the buffalos
And delicate as butterflies.
As they feed, elephants strip the bark and leaves from trees.
The elephants trample the grass of the savanna to the ground.

The elephant is Zambia's great compost maker,
But other animals are there to take on the work that he begins.
These are the little ones, millipedes and centipedes,
And ten thousand grubs and worms.
A billion busy ants work day and night
To build again the soil that rains have washed away.

We men and women, children too, must take great care.
Great care of all our compost makers.
We must give respect to great and small
Even as we give respect to elders and to chiefs.

Oh! Elephant and millipede, Oh! Buffalo and butterfly
You made the soil for all our ancestors.
You are making it now for our children and our children's
children.
We sing a song of praise to you
And thank the God of all created things.

Ennias Michello
Diocese of Monze, Sustainable Agriculture Programme
Chief's training Evaluation Workshop
17-12 April 1994

INTRODUCTION

In the last half century as the winds of change have swept through Africa nothing has been left as it was before.

Amongst the trees that fell in the hurricane were the white missionaries. Many rural Africans would like to see them return, if for no other reason than that it would remind them of the comparative peace, order and prosperity of colonial days. But we old missionaries know that can never be, for we know that along with some good things we managed to do we did much harm and made unwittingly some dreadful mistakes. With all white men of our time we made the arrogant assumption that we, and we alone had the the truth, the whole truth, and nothing but the truth, and that everything African, all their ancient culture, all their ways and wisdom were inferior to ours. One of our great mistakes, for example, was to encourage them to believe that only through the gateway of our Western form of education could we lead them out of their poverty, ignorance and disease, into the social, political and economic freedom which we claimed was ours.

It was a false hope, a spurious freedom. Our task as members of a 'missionary' church today is to admit to our folly and begin as crestfallen equals to work alongside the people of Africa as they rediscover the riches of their culture, restore fertility of their land and liberate themselves from the powerful economic forces which drove them into the soul destroying treadmill of international trade.

In that half century my life has been interwoven with the lives of the people of Zambia. Of all those fifty-five turbulent years which have seen Zambia pass from Colonial dependency, through independence and back to pauper dependency on foreign aid, none have meant more to me than the eight years I spent living in the village of Chipapa.

To only a favoured few is given the privilege of sharing so intimately the lives of a people whose culture is so radically different from their own, and it was in Chipapa during those years when I worked with them, and sat round their fires to talk with them that I began to feel the heartbeat of a different Africa. In the end it was an experience which turned my life upside down, because for the first time I began to see it from the underside, looking up through peasant eyes and it is this topsy-turvy revelation that I want to share with others.

This was the essential core of all my African experience and it seems to me that there is no better way to share it than to invite you to stand at my shoulder as I turn the pages of the diary in which I recorded what was happening to me at that time and what I felt about it all.

Some explanation is needed before I plunge you into this unfamiliar world, because you must be asking, Who is this man? This Englishman who went at the age of fifty to live in an African village? Why did he go? And where was the village and who were the people who lived there?

In attempting to answer these questions I start my book by telling you in a fragmentary way the story of my own journey, from the moment I stepped out of the train at Lusaka station in 1943 carrying my khaki pith helmet and my white man's baggage until my return on a Boeing 707 at Heathrow in 1974 carrying a straw hat, a presentation copper tray from President Kaunda and a carved wooden stool, but leaving my heart behind me.

Then I tell Chipapa's story by recounting what I heard from the lips of an old man Shachifwa from his birth in 1902 until the day we first met in 1966 and journeyed on together.

Although I thought when I left Africa in 1974 that I would

never see Chipapa again I was mistaken, and the final pages of my book tell of other brief visits to the village.

I had set out in 1989 with a bicycle and a dream that one day there would be at least one organic farm family in every village in Africa. I lost the bike in the deep bush of the Zambezi valley, but the dream lived on. Six years have passed with little apparent change, indeed after two terrible droughts some things have gone from bad to worse. But the silent waters of an organic revolution have been gathering in the creeks and inlets and everywhere there are signs that the tide is turning. All but purblind African ministries of Agriculture and rapacious chemical companies have accepted the folly and stupidities of the so called 'Green Revolution'. Everywhere I go I find people desperately looking for an alternative form of agriculture which will enable them to feed themselves and restore fertility to their relentlessly eroding land.

The voices of Fritz Schumaker, Lawrence Hills, Bill Mollison and other organic prophets are no longer cries in the wilderness. The technology required for the development of sustainable agriculture is now understood. We know that soil erosion can be prevented by planting the right varieties of trees and vetever grass in the right way in the right places at the right time. We know for example that a chisel plough is a far more soil- friendly tool than a mould board plough in hot arid areas, and that in most circumstances a thousand little hand-made conservation dams are better than a mega-dam for harvesting water in the rains.

At last we have begun to ask the right questions and we are finding answers. Now we can see clearly why things have gone so terribly wrong as a result of our misuse of the land. We know the technical answers; what is now lacking is the means of spreading the knowledge of appropriate technologies throughout the entire population. Everyone, Mercedes-driven politicians and office-bound civil servants, teachers and students in agriculture colleges and schools, religious leaders, illiterate men and women in the remotest villages need to hear the good news. Unquestionably the most effective way of getting the message across is to enable people to see with their own eyes what happens to their land and their lives when they begin to farm organically.

The driving force behind the organic revolution is the peasant farmers' disillusionment with the promise that the use of artificial fertilizers and hybrid seed would make them all rich. Zambia's agriculture became hooked on chemical fertilizers thirty years ago, little wonder that her people are suffering from the traumatic withdrawal symptoms of this destructive national addiction! Nevertheless in the most unlikely places signs of hope are appearing. No one could claim that the organic revolution is sweeping like wildfire through the African bush, but it smoulders almost everywhere and little fires are waiting to burst into flame. Six years ago I thought it was my job to light the fire, but I found it already burning. I realised then that all I had to do was to bend down and blow on the sparks wherever I could find them.

Most encouraging of all is to see how the organic revolution is now firmly in the hands of a growing number of well trained competent and dedicated men and women in Zambia. For example in the Southern Province, Ennias Michelo, senior agricultural officer of the Roman Catholic Diocese of Monze has been running courses on organics for farmers, village headmen, chiefs, agricultural extension officers, community development workers, teachers and especially leaders of women's groups. He always starts his permaculture courses with a sermon, which uses the good African practice of question and

4

answer. It goes like this:-

Q"Who was Adam?"	A "The first man"
Q"Who was Eve?"	A "The first woman"
Q"Where did they live?"	A "In the Garden of Eden"
Q"Where is Adam now?"	A Silence
Q"Where is Eve now?"	A Silence
Q"Where is the garden?"	A Silence

"Now" says Ennias, "I will give you the answers to the questions you have failed".

He points to a man and says, "You are Adam".

He points to a woman and says, "You are Eve".

"Where is Eden? It is here, it is your own garden where you grow your maize and sorghum and millet and pumpkins and water melons and the calabashes you use for cups to drink your beer. Who gave Adam and Eve their garden? God gave them His garden and told them to look after it for Him. God has given you your gardens. Are you looking after them properly? Do you make contour ridges on cleared land to stop the soil washing away in heavy rain? Do you put manure from your cattle kraals on your fields? Do you try to plant maize every year in the same place without also growing beans and sunn hemp? Why do you complain to God that He has given you poorer and poorer harvests each year until your soil becomes useless? Don't blame God. It is your own fault because you do not keep the agreement with God to look after the land He gave you".

One of the lectures which he gave in 1994 to the Diocese of Monze Sustainable Agriculture Programme Chiefs' Training Evaluation Workshop reads like a creation hymn. It is from his poem "The Compost Makers" that I have taken the title of this little book which is dedicated to him and all Zambia's farmers and growers.

5

CHAPTER 1
My Story 1943 - 1966

Carrying the white man's burden

In the middle of World War II, I being a minister of the Methodist Church was in a 'reserved occupation' and so permitted to serve as a missionary in a British colony. Many colonial administrators were on active service and missionaries who had always been their allies running schools and clinics in the bush were encouraged to keep these services to the 'natives' functioning properly.

I was appointed to Northern Rhodesia, now Zambia, where I became missionary and manager of schools to an area half the size of Wales, where the District Commissioner was a man who had been brought out of retirement to hold the fort until a younger man came back from the war. He was a colonial servant of the old school, a patrician who went on tour wearing hunting jacket, jodhpurs and white kid gloves. He made his journeys on a bicycle with a District Messenger running beside him. When they came to an incline on the forest track where the old man found difficulty in keeping the pedals turning the Messenger would insert a forked stick under the saddle and gently push man and bike up the slope.

We two Christian Englishmen felt it our duty to carry the white man's burden and bring all the benefits of western civilisation to a people who seemed to have emerged only recently from the Stone Age. It is quite painful for me to look back on those early years of missionary service. I did not realise it at the time but I had been so influenced by my fellow missionaries that I allowed myself to slip all too easily into the belief that African people with their culture and life style were a 'backward' people who needed 'advancement'. It appals me to think how as a young man of 25 I took my place alongside the District Commissioner to control and order the lives of forty thousand fellow human beings. The District Commissioner was in charge of law and order and all the administration of good government. I was in charge of the church and the fifteen mission schools and was expected to convert them from their old beliefs to Christianity.

Learning to speak the language

Not being a natural linguist I was having great difficulty in understanding and speaking the local language. In desperation I went to live for a while in one of the villages thirty miles away from the mission, where no-one spoke English and where I could immerse myself in the sound of chatter round the cooking fires and observe the body language of the people who surrounded me all day. The hours were long and tedious as I sat on the stool they gave me in the shade of the headman's house, collecting in my little notebook the names of all the things around me, like the words for cooking pot and firewood, maize meal and all the different kinds of 'relish' such as wild spinach, pumpkin leaves, ground nuts and sour milk which was always eaten with the stiff and stodgy 'porridge', which is their staple food.

I learned to use a native adze and carved a six foot wooden cross which I set up by the well. There was a deaf and dumb blacksmith in a neighbouring village so I went to visit him and bought an iron spearhead which he had fashioned out of an old car spring, using a short length of railway line as an anvil and blowing up his charcoal fire with goat skin bellows, worked by his eight year old son.

When I got back to my village I hammered the spearhead into the cross and asked a visiting preacher to explain to the mystified villagers that on such a cross had Jesus their Saviour been crucified and the spear was man's sin which had been the cause of his death. I planted zinnia seeds at the foot of the cross and some of the women helped to gather thorn bushes to make a fence round the little garden to keep cattle and goats away. I heard later that soon after I left someone stole the spear, the flowers died from lack of water and the white ants ate the cross. I had a lot more to learn than the language.

I had not been on my mission station at Nambala for more than a couple of years before I began to question the educational policy of the Missionary Society. This aimed to give a basic education for four years in literacy and numeracy in our fifteen village primary schools, then select the thirty best pupils and bring them in for a further two years education at the central mission boarding school. At that stage a few were selected for another three years to go to the 'Upper School' after which they were ready for vocational training as teachers, medical workers, veterinary assistants, agricultural assistants or government clerical workers.

A rural training centre for school drop-outs

It was a deliberate policy to produce Christian leadership for the country but it did nothing to give the mass of pupils in the primary schools an education which would fit them for developing a better life in the villages.

It was then I had what I thought was a great idea. I would start a Rural Training Centre on the mission to give a two year training course to twenty drop-out youths, (NB it never crossed my mind to offer training to girls), in building, carpentry and farming. If they had these skills, I argued, they would not drift to the towns in search of work but stay to improve the villages. They enjoyed the building and carpentry but hated the farming which they regarded as women's work. At the end of their training they demanded certificates and all went off to Lusaka where they immediately found paid employment as bricklayers and joiners. That was the end of my first attempt to halt the 'drift to the towns'.

The black man fears that the white man will steal the land

In our rural isolation we were unaware of the 'winds of change' which were beginning to sweep across Africa, but I was becoming aware of how deeply resentful the people were of the coming of the white man to take up farms along the line of rail. I had an indication of the depth of their fears when the government Department of Water Affairs sent a white water engineer to supervise teams of well diggers in the villages. It was a three year programme so this man, who had a wife and child, decided to build a small thatched house from sun dried brick rather than live in a tent. The rumour quickly spread that he was a government spy who had been sent to find out where there was good land which would be given to white settlers.

As part of a programme of land conservation to prevent soil erosion, the government helped African peasant farmers to construct contour ridges. It started well but again a rumour began to spread that once the peasants had made the ridges, Boer farmers would move in to take the land. Chief Shakumbila's area, south of the Mission was the worst affected and as I was manager of a primary school near the chief's court and knew him well, I was sent with Unwin Moffat the provincial agricultural officer to quash this rumour. A big meeting was called. The Chief sat on his stool in the shade of a giant wild fig with one hundred and fifty peasant farmers gathered round him seated on the ground. They had come on their bicycles which they parked under the surrounding trees but not before they had

9

taken care to remove the bicycle pumps from the clips under the cross bars and stuff them down the backs of their shirts with the pump handles protruding at the neck.

Through the official government interpreter, Unwin Moffat explained how important it was to continue making contour ridges because otherwise all the top soil would be washed away, and it would not be possible to grow any food crops at all. He said that for the good of the people the government had introduced a Native Authority Ordinance which would force all farmers to make ridges and keep them in good repair. If they refused to do so Chief Shakumbila would impose a heavy fine.

When he had finished his speech Moffat sat down by the side of the Chief. There was silence at first, then the farmers began to mutter amongst themselves and the muttering swelled into an angry chorus of dissent. Then to a man they all stood up and drawing their cycle pumps from their shirt collars like bayonets from their scabbards they waved them in the air shouting "Twakaka, twakaka. we refuse, we refuse". They gathered up their cycles from under the trees and rode away leaving the Chief, Unwin Moffat and me to reflect on the Sala's defiant audacity and the government's total impotence in the face of it.

"There must be political trouble-makers abroad", said the District Commissioner when we returned to the Boma. And they were spreading another vicious rumour. It was being said that the Europeans were contaminating all the sugar being sold in the village shops with an invisible powder which when taken, even in small quantities with your tea or mealie meal porridge would cause infertility in men and cause women to abort. This was a device used by Europeans to wipe out the African race so that they could take all the land for themselves. I went to see Chief Moono who lived only a few miles away from the mission, to ask whether he had heard the rumour. "Oh yes" he said, "I believe it is true and most of my people have stopped taking sugar. But I shan't stop having it in my tea because I have got enough children already".

Bible greasers

One Sunday afternoon I was having tea with my family under the great wild fig tree in my garden, when a man appeared out of the surrounding bush and came over to the tea table. I was deeply affronted because everyone on the mission station knew that Sunday afternoons were sacrosanct and no-one should be allowed to disturb the missionary at this time.

The stranger was dressed in a ragged shirt with grubby khaki trousers and he wore no shoes on his dusty feet. He gave me none of the usual courteous African greetings but silently handed me a letter written in pencil on the lined paper of a single page torn from a school exercise book.

"Dear Muluti (meaning 'teacher') we know that you missionaries have been sent here by the government to apply Bible grease. You have come to make us soft so that we will not oppose Colonial rule. You will never succeed because we African people will take power and you with all the other white people will be thrown out of the country ...."

Then as silently as he came he melted away amongst the trees beyond the tall spiked sisal bushes which surrounded the mission station. I did not see him again until the day of the District Agricultural Show when the Colonial Governor came out from Lusaka to show the flag. All the chiefs and their councillors gathered to welcome the Governor. They were an unimpressive group of men dressed up in ill fitting secondhand lounge suits and wearing a variety of hats from bowlers to feather-bedecked trilbies. The only exception was Chief Chibuluma who wore his traditional leopard skins.

The governor in his gleaming white uniform with gold-braided epaulettes and plumed helmet was an imposing figure. He was accompanied by the silver band of the Northern Rhodesia Police and when they struck up the strains of "God Save The Queen" the District Commissioner and I stood shoulder to shoulder with him on the show ground dais.

After the opening ceremony I wandered off to mingle with the crowds and behind one of the hastily erected stalls I was accosted once again by the man who had called me a "Bible greaser". This time he delivered, not a letter, but a small brown paper parcel which felt almost like a bag of coins but it was too light to be money. I tore it open and saw the glitter of about a hundred gilded tokens which I recognised as the little medals which I as Manager of Schools, had issued for distribution to all children in our mission schools to commemorate the coronation of Queen Elizabeth II.

Then the man spoke to me and said,

"We are telling you to take back these medals to your Queen in England and tell her that we do not recognise her as our ruler. Mr Harry Nkumbula, the National President of the African National Congress of Northern Rhodesia is the true leader of this country."

Then he disappeared into the crowd and I was left holding the medals in my hand and wondering what I should do. One of the Governors's staff came to tell me that it was my turn to meet him for an informal chat about the work of the Methodist Mission in the District. I told the Governor about the return of the medals - after all he was the Queen's representative and would know what should be done about such a horrendous insult. But he seemed to laugh it off.

"Don't worry, young man" he said, "I've heard that there are one or two of these chaps around who are beginning to get a bit too big for their boots. You don't need to concern yourself, I can assure you we have the situation totally in control. I'll ask the District Commissioner to get his Messengers to find out who this chap is and we'll make arrangement to have him followed. We'll soon put a stop to all this nonsense."

(Many years later I was to learn that my mysterious visitor was Edward Liso Mungoni who became one of Zambia's most highly respected politicians and a member of the Anglican Church.)

Apartheid

In 1955 I left Nambala mission and was appointed General Secretary of the United Society for Christian Literature in Northern Rhodesia. My brief was to travel the length and breadth of the country (which is twice the size of Britain,) with a Landrover book-van. I was based at Kitwe on the Copperbelt where I had my first encounter with white racism. Most of the white men who worked the copper mines had come from the Republic of South Africa and they brought with them the doctrine of 'apartheid' or 'separate development' which was applied even more rigorously than in Johannesburg or Capetown.

My children attended a school for white boys and girls only, my wife went shopping in stores which had separate counters for serving either whites or blacks. The bread, tea, milk and sugar were all the same. The money was the same money for all, but the black and white never talked to one another. When the circus came to town all the ring-side seats were reserved for whites while the blacks stood in a separate enclosure at the back. On Sundays all the Christians worshipped the same God, sang the same hymns, read the same Bible but each race prayed in its own church.

13

When a fellow black Christian travelled with me in the Landrover and I stopped for a cup of tea and a plate of fish and chips at a roadside cafe I could not invite him in to share the meal with me. The proprietor would simply refuse to serve him, not even allowing him to have a cup of tea outside on the verandah lest he 'contaminate' the cups which were kept for the use of Europeans only. It was all so stupid, so unnecessary, and I knew it was wrong.

White man joins black man's political party

We moved to Lusaka, and when I heard that Kenneth Kaunda, the leader of the United National Independence Party (U.N.I.P.) had been released from a spell as a political prisoner I invited him into my house. My white colleagues shook their heads in disapproval when they saw a fellow missionary getting mixed up in politics which they regarded as a dirty and inevitably violent game. However, for me the issue had become crystal clear. The struggle for power between black and white had begun. The only question was whether whites could be persuaded to hand over their power without the threat of violence. Kaunda, who had been deeply influenced by the teachings of Mahatma Ghandi announced a campaign of non-violence to achieve independence for his people. I said I would join him in the campaign because I too believed that non-violent direct action was right, and I would do my best as a whiteman to persuade the British government that the time had come to give parity to blacks in the legislative council in preparation for the day when they would achieve complete independence.

During the next seven years I continued to travel the country with books in my Landrover but also began to take an active part in politics. My first venture was to publish and distribute a cheap edition of "The Power of Non-Violence" a little

14

paperback written by an English Quaker. I arranged for it to be translated into two of the major local languages and I like to think it played a part in helping to keep the struggle for independence free from the worst excesses of racial hatred and bitterness.

During these years most of the churches and their ministers stood aloof from the struggle, believing that their task was to keep out of politics. I agreed that the church as an institution should not make political pronouncement, but Christian individuals would soon be given the vote and they would have to decide for themselves whether they should become Nationalists or Federalists. I also knew that Kaunda was being misunderstood and misrepresented in the white dominated newspapers, which consistently portrayed him as a dangerous and violent man.

Somehow I persuaded the London based committee of my Society (USCL) to put up the money for the publication of a book dealing with the red-hot issue of 'Christianity and Politics'. I knew I had to work fast, so I invited Kaunda, the most prominent politician of the day, loved by blacks and hated by whites to meet with the Reverend Colin Morris, the radical Methodist minister of the Chingola church on the Copperbelt. For a whole day they sat together, engaged in a profound dialogue, which I then published under the title "Black Government?". I printed an edition of 2000 which sold like hot cakes, partly because the vendors were given credit and a fair discount. A good number pocketed the proceeds of their sales and disappeared without trace, leaving us to write off a substantial debt as the USCL Society's contribution to the cause of justice and peace in Central Africa!

As I came to know Kaunda more intimately I began to realise how difficult it was becoming for him to hold fast to his belief in the 'Power of Non-Violence'. It was not enough for me to publish books on the subject, I had to come out into the open and join the United National Independence Party (U.N.I.P). At first he advised me not to 'go public' because of the repercussions on my family. He promised to keep my membership card locked up in the U.N.I.P. safe along with the cards of the other five or six Europeans who held secret membership.

But as I heard more and more people of my race vilify and misrepresent this man whom I had come to respect for his ability, integrity and total commitment to the cause of non racial democratic government, I felt unable to hold my peace. With his permission, one Saturday afternoon I joined a U.N.I.P. rally in an African township on the edge of Lusaka and from the top of an ant hill addressed a crowd of cheering U.N.I.P. supporters. I can remember very little of what I said, but I do remember seeing one of the white policemen who had come to control the crowd take a tape recorder out of his pocket when I said "no taxation without representation". The next day the headline in the Sunday paper screamed, "Arm waving parson stirs the crowd to violence". I then knew that there was no turning back.

The founding of the Zambia Youth Service

I became an active worker for the UNIP cause and in 1963 Kaunda asked me to help in setting up the Zambia Youth Service with the objective of gathering the unemployed youths from the streets of Lusaka and the Copperbelt, putting them into training camps and turning them into disciplined citizens of the new nation. He appointed me deputy director.

We started well and it was not long before there were over a thousand young men and a few women marching round in forest green uniforms being told that the future of the nation lay in their hands. I well remember the day when the African Director of the Zambia Youth Service (ZYS) came to the formal opening of our new camp in Kitwe.

"This is a pilot project". he said "You have been recruited by Kaunda the President of our new nation to set an example to all youth and lead them into a new era of independence and prosperity".

He then left with his entourage of ZYS officers to return to national H.Q. and I remained to encourage the youths to get on with the unexciting task of clearing the bush and digging the soil with their hoes in preparation for planting their food crops. Soon after the Director's visit I received a delegation of youths who asked me how long it would be before they started their training as 'pilots' in the Zambia Air Force. It was an understandable mistake, because with all the euphoria that surrounded Zambia's declaration of independence the gap between dream and reality had grown out of all proportion. But on October 24th that memorable day in 1964 when at the great stadium in Lusaka the Union Jack came fluttering down and the green, black and orange flag of Zambia streamed out against the sky, Kaunda our new President stood at the salute as the young men and women of the Zambia Youth Service marched proudly by.

In the heavy rains of 1965 the youths who were housed in temporary grass shelters and leaking tents refused to hoe the soggy ground and demanded tractors. When I told them there would be no tractors they rioted and not unnaturally blamed me for causing their discontent. I was relieved of my duties and left to kick my heels while a commission of enquiry looked into the problems of the Youth Service. Although I was finally exonerated from all blame except unbelievable naivety, I was not asked to continue as Deputy Director of the Youth Service.

I become a Land Settlement Officer

One day I was invited by the President to accompany him on a tour of the remote rural area of Kasempa. At a gathering of chiefs he announced that he had appointed me to set up a Board of National Re-settlement. The fact that he had forgotten to inform me seemed not to worry him at all and on the plane coming home he simply told me that I should report to the appropriate Ministry the following day.

In those chaotic days under the benevolent dictatorship of a charismatic leader all things seemed possible. We thought that given the money and the power and plenty of bright ideas we could develop a country from the top down. My minister was a recently reformed freedom fighter who had shown great ability in delivering passionate political speeches to large crowds from the tops of ant hills on the Copperbelt, but knew even less about land re-settlement than I did.

He worked out for himself, with a good deal of encouragement from his 'comrades in the struggle,' that there was only one way to lift the rural masses out of their poverty and stop the universal drift away from the villages into the towns. Every one of Zambia's thirty rural districts should have their own 'Rural Service Centres' where the government would provide all the facilities available in towns - secondary schools, hospitals, modern housing with piped water, shops and plenty of electricity to provide bright light all night long. People would leave their villages and congregate in these havens of delight. He gave instructions to all the newly appointed African District Governors to go out with their officials into the bush in their sparkling new Landrovers to choose suitable sites for these centres.

As soon as news arrived in our Lusaka office that a place had been selected, the minister would order a government plane to take us out to the nearest air strip where we were met by the local Governor and the officers of all the departments of education, health, agriculture, local government, water affairs, public works, police, game and fisheries. We advanced in convoy along a track which had been hurriedly hacked through the bush to a clearing in the trees to which the local chief and his followers had been summoned. The minister would make a long speech which had been written for him well in advance and we always made sure that we had with us a broadcasting officer so that his speech was given a prominent place that night in the national news bulletin, thus maintaining the illusion that the government of the people which had been elected by the people was indeed caring for the deepest needs of the people.

People themselves were never asked whether they wanted to leave their villages and move away from their gardens and their grazing lands into these centres. The men who had won political independence for their country were quite sure in their own minds that they knew best what was good for their people, and they genuinely believed that the copper mines had made Zambia so rich that there was limitless money available for the government to supply anything they asked for.

The Re-Settlement Board met to receive reports of the selected sites and it was suggested that before the minister, its chairman, could fulfil his promises to the people it would be necessary to do a few more survey and planning and feasibility studies. This would require assistance from the planning officers of all the other ministries, who replied that many European technical officers had left the country at the time Zambia became independent, very few Africans had been trained to replace them, they had more than enough work to do developing their own unrealistic projects so they were sorry but they could not help.

Lurking in the corridors of the Ministry of Rural Development were people of many nations on the look out for the lucrative contacts always available in such situations. Amongst them were Greeks from Doxiadis Ltd the world famous company of town and country planners. They saw no problem, they would fly out immediately all the technical experts required to survey and plan one Rural Service Centre in each of Zambia's eight provinces. They made quick estimates of what the whole exercise would cost, demanded a substantial sum in advance and flew home to Athens. They did not tell the minister how long it would take to prepare the plans, so while he waited he found plenty of political work to fill up his time. In the event it took Doxiadis two and a half years to produce their elaborate, totally impractical and exorbitantly costly plans, none of which was ever implemented.

I worked all day from my little office on the fourth floor of the Ministry of Rural Development, as part of a small team of agricultural economists, land use advisers, agronomists, statisticians and foreign experts who had been brought in to devise Zambia's five year development plan. We were under constant pressure from our political masters to bring about an instant agrarian revolution which would transform the peasantry, who had for centuries lived more or less successfully at subsistence level, into modern cash crop farmers.

They were stirring times. A fleet of six hundred tractors was ordered from overseas. A fertilizer factory was built on the Kafue River. Hundreds of bags of hybrid high yielding maize seed were imported from the south and a Land Bank was set up to provide agricultural credit. The so called 'Green Revolution' had begun.

A doctor's mistaken identity

One day in 1966 a telephone call came through from State House to say that there was an eminent German economist Dr. Priebe who would like to talk to me. President Kaunda had invited him to visit Zambia to advise on the question of the dispersal of industry into rural areas. When he came on the phone he said:

"I have been in Zambia for two weeks, and I have had the presidential plane to fly me around wherever I wanted to go. I have visited every province; I have had conferences and discussions with everyone from the Minister of Commerce and Industry and the Director of the Department of Agriculture to the Mayor of the City Council and the Chief Engineer, but I have never actually set foot in a Zambian village, and I am leaving on the plane tomorrow. Could you possibly take me out, even if it is only for half an hour to an ordinary typical African village?"

It was not an easy question to answer, because there are no African villages left round the city. The white settlers forty years ago had taken care of that. They had moved the Africans into 'Reserves' and taken their land to make their own large farms. But then I remembered that seventeen miles to the south-east of the city is the village of Chipapa where Daniel Kalambalala, a retired Methodist evangelist had gone to live and he had once sent me a message begging me to fetch his small son Chipo who was dangerously ill and bring him into hospital. It had taken me a long time to find the place which by city standards is quite off the map, and when I finally reached the village down at the end of a dusty earth track, all I found was a decaying rural slum. What better place, I thought to take the German doctor. I might even be able to puncture some of his romantic dreams of a happy and contented people living in sweet little thatched cottages with blue smoke curling into the sky, where old men puff their pipes through the lazy day, the women dance by moonlight, and the night is filled with the rhythmic beat of drums and children's songs.

A baby in a bundle of rags

We arrived in the early afternoon. The people brought stools and a cow-hide deck chair for us to sit on. They just sat on the bare ground. The conversation began slowly.

"How are you all in the town?" they asked.

"Very well thank you, and how are you here in the village?"

"Very well thank you, and what are you eating up in the town?"

"Not so bad thank you, and what are you eating here?"

"We have nothing to eat. Our stomachs are empty, there is only hunger here."

Then in their misery they began to pour out their troubles. "Oh Muluti, we are in despair in this place. Many oxen have died so that we could only plough half the land. When we finished ploughing all the seed was eaten up by the partridges, and at the time of weeding many women fell sick so the weeds choked all the growing plants, and then we had five weeks without rain and all the plants died. When it came to harvest all the ox-carts got broken so we could not carry the cobs to our grain bins, and the white ants ate them where they lay on the ground."

The village street had not been swept for months and piles of rubbish littered all the scuffled ground. There were gaping holes in the rotten thatch of the roofs, and all the chicken houses were tumbling down. From behind a ruined hut came a woman carrying a bundle of rags. In it was a child too weak to cry, a tiny thing of skin and bone with hollow eyes which looked at us in wonderment from just this side of death. The woman had heard me introduce the professor by the name of 'doctor', and so she had come to him for help.

"Perhaps the doctor has brought some medicine in his bag to heal the child?"

"No, he is not that kind of doctor and all he has got in his bag is a camera. But what is wrong?" I asked.

With one hand the woman drew aside the bodice of her ragged dress revealing an abcess as big as a coffee saucer on her left breast. In her other hand she held a baby's feeding bottle with a filthy rubber teat. The bottle was full of a grey liquid in which floated little lumps of stale and undissolved milk powder.

"No he is not that kind of doctor" I repeated, "he is not a doctor of medicine he is a doctor of agriculture, economics and planning."

I suggested that perhaps she might like to come back with us in the car to the hospital in Lusaka. But the woman just wrapped up her bundle of rags and walked away to her house. She knew it was already too late, and that the time had come for her to find a quiet place, a patch of ground beneath a forest tree where she and her mother could dig a little grave, and bury their tiny child.

The doctor was taken back to Lusaka to catch his flight to Germany, Daniel went back to his house and I climbed to the top of the little hill above the village. There I had a dream of another Chipapa, and another Daniel, and another child. Below me all along the lake shore I saw fat cattle grazing, and I heard the voices of a hundred families all busy in the fields, and there was Daniel riding home on his ox-cart, piled so high with cobs of golden maize that he didn't even bother to stop when some of them spilled off along the way. A small boy came laughing up the hill and sat down beside me on a little rock. He put his hand into my hand and as we sat there he never tried to take it away.

It is at this point in my story that 'Chipapa' needs to be put into its historical and geographical context. This can best be done by telling old Shachifwa's story. He was the senior headman of the seven scattered family clans which occupy the land around Chipapa's little hill.

CHAPTER 2
Shachifwa's Story

Sometime about 1900 Shachifwa was born in Chipapa, a village not far off the wagon road which brought the first white traders, missionaries and prospectors from South Africa crossing the Zambezi at Walker's Drift and entering the country they called 'the far north'.

He spent his childhood in the village playing with the other children and helping his mother weeding the scattered crop of maize in the 'garden', scaring the birds off the millet and the sorghum and watching his father's little herd of scrawny cattle. Sometimes he was taken to the Big Road to see the jolting wagons passing by. It was an impressive sight for a child. Sixteen oxen, two by two straining in their heavy wooden yokes as they dragged their wagons through rutted sand in the dry season and churning mud in the rains. In front of the team walked a young boy whom they called a 'voor looper' (the dew scatterer) and beside them came the driver cracking his forty foot whip of rawhide. Sometimes on the wooden bench up front there might be a 'muzungu' (a white man,) though to the naked eye the dark tanned skin of his face and forearms would make him more brown than white.

The dream of Cecil Rhodes

Before Shachifwa was born in Chipapa, Cecil Rhodes in Johannesburg had dreamed of the map of Africa painted imperial red from Cape Town to Cairo. If the dream was to come true he would have to build a bridge across the Zambezi, and he knew that the ox wagons of his Great North Road (it is still called Cairo Road where it runs as the main highway through Lusaka), would have to be replaced with a railway line. How else would the copper from the mines at Katanga in the

Congo be carried south to the Cape for onward shipment to the markets of Europe, America and the Far East? How else could coal be carried from the Wankie collieries in Rhodesia to the Congo. How else would the woollen blankets and cotton cloth of the Yorkshire and Lancashire mills be brought in to exchange for the labour of workers who mined the rich ore bodies of copper which were being discovered in the north?

First train across the Victoria Falls

The railway reached the Victoria Falls in 1904. Cecil Rhodes had died in 1902 but before he died he ordered that the bridge should be built so close to the Falls that the spray should be blown over the trains, and this was done. The native people who were working there prophesied that when the first train went on the bridge it would fall off down into the river below.

They watched expectantly as the first train came, and cheered when a leopard leaped in front of it, but the train never stopped. It steamed on, its cow-catcher grid caught the leopard on the shoulder hurling it down into the seething cauldron below the falls. The white men laughed in triumph but the people said the reason why the train had not fallen was because it had become wise and had killed the leopard as an offering to the spirit of the falls whose name was 'mosi-wa-tunya' (the smoke that thunders) long before Livingstone named it after Victoria, his white queen.

Shachifwa, as soon as he was strong enough to wield an axe and use a pick and shovel, was recruited by Rhodesia Railways Ltd. to work in one of the many labour gangs which were being employed to clear the line for the laying of the track to the north after the bridge was built at Victoria Falls. Each man was given a weekly ration of food and after three months of hard labour a voucher which could be used in a white trader's store to

26

exchange for a blanket or a length of blue cotton cloth to take home to his wife, or cast iron cooking pots, candles, matches, soap, combs and mirrors.

At that time the North Western Territory of Rhodesia was administered by the officials of The British South Africa Chartered Company (BSA) to which paramount chief Lewanika had ceded all mineral and trading rights over an area almost twice the size of Great Britain. The BSA needed money to pay their administrators and the police force which was required to maintain the law and order needed if they were to trade in peace.

The Hut Tax

This revenue could be obtained from mining royalties, sale of land, custom duties, postal charges, and other sources. These sources did not bring in enough money. The obvious answer was taxation. The new white settlers were not taxed but the company saw nothing wrong with taxing the black inhabitants of the land they had annexed. So in 1904 they introduced a hut-tax which was levied on men and all their wives except the first. In the early days the tax could be paid in goods such as gold, copper, ivory, livestock, cotton, coffee and salt. These goods were each given a value: for instance an ox was worth 15/-, a sheep 4/- and a chicken 3d. Later the tax could be paid only in cash, the hope being to draw the people into a cash economy. The annual tax was between 5/- and 10/- and if a man did not pay he had to work for four months instead.

So it was that the problem of raising revenue from taxation became linked with the problem of labour. Villagers watched as all the able bodied men packed their blanket rolls and trekked off bare footed to the white man's mines and farms. The old men, the women and the children who were left behind had hardly strength enough to grow food for themselves let alone provide maize meal needed for the young men working underground on the Copperbelt.

Land sold to white farmers

So here was the problem of shortage of food for the miners and shortage of revenue from the hut tax. Then some white man in the employ of the BSA company had a brilliant idea that he claimed would kill these two birds with a single well aimed stone. His plan, quite breathtaking in its white colonial audacity, would have far reaching consequences for the future of the black owners of the land. It would change for ever the life of Shachifwa and his village of Chipapa.

He traced two long lines on his map each running roughly parallel to the red line of rail, about twenty or thirty miles east and west of it. He explained how all the people living along the railway would be pushed sideways to settle as best they could in what would be called 'Native Reserves'. The land thus emptied of its age old inhabitants would be demarcated in parcels measuring anything from two thousand to five thousand acres. This would be offered for sale at sixpence an acre to any white man who wished to apply for a farm. Some would come from Britain but most would move up from the south. Boer farmers from the Transvaal who went north after the Anglo-Boer war would come in their ox wagons with their cattle, their donkeys, their chickens, their ploughs and their wives and children. These Boers employed poor whites known as 'Bywoners' who lived in mud huts and gave a third of their produce to the 'baas' for whom they worked.

The BSA Company would earn a pretty penny from the sale of the land but that would be as nothing compared to the revenue that would pour into their empty coffers from hut tax paid by thousands of new wage earners. The pioneer farmers would need great labour gangs to cut down trees to clear the land for the plough. They would draw them from the reservoirs of labour created by the establishment of the Native Reserves. The natives would have to leave their families behind in the new villages of the Reserve and come to live in compounds on the farms in the same way as labourers in the north left their villages to work on the copper mines.

Expropriation of Chipapa's lands

In 1929 Chipapa's people were forced to join the exodus and they were pushed back into the narrow valley which runs down between the Lusaka escarpment and the Mpande hills above the Kafue Gorge. Shachifwa returned from labouring on the railway to help his people construct new huts and clear a small patch of ground for them to plant a little sorghum and millet and a few sweet potatoes. He worked with others cutting bush poles to construct a kraal for the headman's herd of cattle and goats and then he went off to look for work on the new farms opening up in the south. The land from which his people had been evicted was no more than small patches of fertile soil scattered amongst the broken hill country which lies between the railway and the low line of the Mpande hills. This land was put up for sale by the BSA Company but when white prospective farmers came to see it they took one look and turned away to find farms in less rugged country.

Slash and burn

The Chipapa people had a rough time in exile. They were ba-Sala by tribe but the ba-Soli amongst whom they came to live resented their arrival. They did not like being forced to share their limited natural resources with people of another tribe. Water in the little stream ran almost dry in the cold season. Grazing land was insufficient and the stony soil was so poor that the only way to get a half decent crop of grain was to 'slash and burn' the virgin bush. This method of agriculture is quite adequate if there are only a few people and plenty of virgin land for them to move around in, because when after two or three years your slashed garden looses its fertility, you can move on to slash another one leaving your old garden in the healing hands of mother nature for thirty years or more to regenerate the grasses, the bushes and the trees. But when there are a great number of people and not enough space for them to move around in, 'slash and burn' as a method of food production spells disaster for both the people and their land, causing massive soil erosion because there is no time to allow the natural regeneration of the bush.

It was not easy for Shachifwa to leave his wife and child in the harsh conditions of the new village. Added to all their other hardships was the presence of a pride of lions in the Mpande hills and marauding hyenas and leopards which sometimes came hunting for cattle and goats, leaping right over the fences of their kraal. There were also honey badgers and pythons which came to kill their chickens.

But Shachifwa had no choice. He had to earn money to pay his 10/- tax and to buy things for himself and his wife Esther whom he married in 1924. For a year or two he worked on the farms in the south where in addition to maize some of the Boer farmers were growing cotton and had found that the climate and the soil were good for growing tobacco. The woodlands which they cleared for their fields provided a seemingly limitless supply of timber to stoke the furnaces in the barns where they produced high quality flue-cured virginia tobacco, a commodity for which they could demand a high price on the auction floors of Salisbury in Southern Rhodesia.

However when his father died and he inherited a few cattle

and some goats he returned home. His people were still angry and resentful about the way they had been pushed off their lands. They were not allowed to return to visit the graves of their ancestors, not even the grave of old Chipapa the freed slave who lies buried at the foot of the hill which bears his name. Why should they have to suffer in these harsh barren hills while if they climbed to the top of them they could look back on the old land from which they had been driven and which had remained forgotten and unused for twenty years? No white man had ever come to make a farm and they were not even allowed onto the land to cut bush poles and grass for their houses, or to graze their cattle and goats amongst the thorn trees which had sprung up in the gardens where once they grew their food.

In desperation Shachifwa set off with other headmen to take their complaints to their Chief who lived a two days' journey away through the hills to the east. Chief Nkomesha heard their story in silence then said he was powerless because although his authority extended over all the lands of ba-Soli, he could do nothing about the land which was stolen by the white people. Ever since the British Government had taken over authority from the BSA Company this land had been designated 'Crown Land' for occupation by whites only. No black people could make farms there although black workers could live there temporarily if employed as servants of white farmers or as labourers in the fields or herdsmen or wagon drivers.

The chief suggested that they should wait until the District Commissioner came on tour in the area to collect taxes and hear people's complaints. He might be able to do something because he had the power and might go to the big white chief, The Governor, who then could take the matter to the King George whom white people regarded as Paramount Chief.

The District Commissioner who was harsh but fair

The District Commissioner at that time was an Englishman called Goodfellow who had a reputation as a strict disciplinarian and a harsh man who did not suffer fools gladly. If he should come unexpectedly on a prison gang of tax defaulters sitting smoking dagga (marijuana) in the shade of a tree when they should have been slashing the grass on the 'Boma' lawn, he would give them a tongue lashing as ruthless as any Boer farmer could give. He would usually include in his castigation the suggestion that if they were not prepared to work for him on the ground they had better get up into the trees with their brothers the baboons for that was the place where they belonged.

But Goodfellow's bark was worse than his bite and he also had a reputation as a fair man who would listen to both sides of an argument and make a sensible judgement. He was not kindly but he was just and people respected him for that.

Goodfellow heard the people's complaint. He recognised the injustice in the situation and he started the long difficult legal process of getting the Governor-in-Council to transfer this piece of Crown Land to the Native Reserve. After a sustained battle with the representatives of the white settlers in the council he succeeded and in 1935 Chipapa was declared a reserve. Goodfellow was a man of considerable foresight and knew that if the return of the exiles took place without careful control there would be endless squabbles about sharing out the land for new gardens. The population had almost doubled since they moved so if they continued to grow their crops using the slash and burn method they would quickly destroy their new habitat. The people would have to agree to make a dramatic break with their past and accept all the disciplines and restraints imposed by the continuous growing of crops on the same land year after year with no chance of fallow. Another serious problem was lack of water as there was no perennial stream on the western slopes of the Mpande hills.

Goodfellow called a meeting with all heads of families to which he also invited an experienced agricultural officer. He told the people quite bluntly that the government would do three things.

1. It would help them to site a catchment dam to gather water during the rains, sufficient for their domestic needs, for watering their goats and cattle, but above all for irrigating a small area of land for growing a cash crop of vegetables.
2. It would demarcate land for making permanent gardens and appoint them a resident agricultural extension officer to live in Chipapa.
3. It would build a cattle dip and appoint a veterinary assistant.

In return for this the people must agree to give their free labour to build the earth wall of the dam, make contour ridges in their gardens to stop soil erosion, rotate their maize crop with a legume like beans or sunn hemp and most of all cart the manure from their cattle kraals and spread it on their gardens.

Return to Chipapa

For a people who had never become accustomed to long periods of hard sustained labour it was a huge undertaking but in the end the dam was built. New houses and cattle kraals were constructed; new gardens were cleared by felling thirty foot thorn trees and then digging out their deep roots; crop lands were contoured. On the land set aside for irrigation, four families began to learn all the skills of how to grow vegetables in the dry season and form a co-operative to market them in the town fifteen miles away. They were paid no wages for all their unremitting labour and it is not surprising that the young able bodied men preferred to leave the monotony of the village for the bright lights of the town. There it was not too difficult in those days to get a job as a garden boy, kitchen boy or office orderly making cups of tea on demand for ministers, permanent secretaries, under secretaries, assistant secretaries, clerical officers, assistant clerical officers, and of course themselves.

Shachifwa had a son called Daniel who never had the chance to go to school simply because in his village there was no school to go to. He grew up with the other village boys herding the cattle and helping sometimes in the maize gardens with the hoeing, planting, weeding and harvest. But many days passed when there was little else to do but talk and learn how to beat a drum and dance and sing at funeral wakes and watch his father Shachifwa make prayer at the graves of his ancestors.

The conversion of Daniel

Then one day a missionary came and Daniel was persuaded that he must give up his old 'sinful' ways be converted and become a Christian. He was not alone in being profoundly influenced by the preaching that he heard. Shachifwa said he was too old to change but amazingly Daniel somehow taught himself to read the Bible and it was not long before he began to preach himself. Indeed he became so enthusiastic in his new Faith that he wanted to do nothing else. The missionaries, always on the look out for dedicated young men to spread the Word and teach the catechism to new converts were impressed. Daniel's life was exemplary, he had given up drinking and when he went to funerals it was not to dance but to sing Christian hymns and to pray.

The African missionary church grew as a result of the work of the young men who were trained as teacher - evangelists. They taught in their village schools during the week and went out to preach in the surrounding villages on Sunday. But as the schools developed the teachers found the demands of the children's education to be so great that they had neither the time nor the inclination to be evangelists.

The missionaries also found themselves giving more time to education and less to evangelism so reluctantly, and as a temporary measure, they began to employ local 'village evangelists'. Daniel was chosen to be one of them and after a period of training in Bible teaching and church doctrine he was delighted to be paid a small monthly wage and be given a house on the mission station to do the only thing he wanted to do which was to gather little groups of Christians together in the surrounding villages to preach to them and to sing and pray. He married a local girl who was baptised as Sarah and they had a daughter whom they called Janala and a son Chipo meaning 'gift from God'.

CHAPTER 3
My life in the village

At that time I was living with my family in 'Woodlands' a leafy suburb of Lusaka which had been built in the days before Independence to house an ever growing population of white civil servants, foreign embassy staff and Lusaka's 'European' business community. My four children had reached the limit of education which Zambian schools could provide, so my wife took them to England. Since our house was then too large for a single person I decided to look for a smaller one.

One Saturday morning in 1967 I got on my bike and rode down the Great North Road as far as Chilanga then turned off the tarmac to Chipapa to visit Daniel Kalambalala whom I had not seen since taking the German doctor to see his village. It was one of those years when late rains fail and as I cycled along the rutted road I saw people lining up with clay pots, buckets and plastic jerry cans to collect the daily ration of water from the drought-relief bowsers which the government had sent out to them from the Chilanga town water supply. When I arrived by Chipapa's little hill I saw people digging for water in the cracked mud on the bottom of the dried up dam.

When I found Daniel he was sitting by a little fire with a group of old men squatting on low stools in the meagre shade of Shachifwa's dilapidated mud brick house. They sucked deep draughts of acrid smoke through the long reed stems of their black clay pipes stopping now and again to lift a glowing ember from the fire to drop it accurately in the wide mouthed bowl of the pipe.

I joined in their grumbling conversation and as I listened to the litany of their woes I was moved. I remembered the dream which I had dreamed for Chipapa on the hill top a year ago.

36

Might it one day come true? If so I wanted more than anything else to be a part of it and to be in at the beginning of its realisation. I knew then that I must come and live in Chipapa.

As I cycled back to Lusaka I realised that if I did go to live in Chipapa it would take too long to commute every day by bicycle from the village to my office in town. But I had a little 'sit-up-and-beg' Ford Popular which we had bought new for £400 in 1960 to ferry the children back and forth to morning lessons and afternoon games in their Lusaka schools. The car had a high clearance and would take in its bone-shaking stride the deep ruts and pot holes of the Chipapa road. The journey should not take much more than forty five minutes each way, so until I could afford a bigger car I would make do with the Popular which by reason of its colour we affectionately called 'the coffee pot'.

The following Saturday I borrowed a small caravan from a friend in Lusaka and we towed it down to the village where Daniel and Sarah invited me to park it under the fig tree between their house and Shachifwa's.

When Daniel some months later built himself a new house nearer to the dam, he invited me to move my caravan with him. When the time came for me to go on leave to see my family in England, I gave him £50 to build me a house on the sloping ground above his chicken run and grain bin. He made the sun dried bricks himself, bought a metal door frame and window frame in Lusaka and paid a local man to build the walls. He went out to the Mpande Hills to cut poles and bark string to bind the roof trusses and Sarah went out with the village women to cut bundles of thatching grass. When I returned some months later there was a beautiful two roomed house measuring inside 12ft. x 10ft., a palace for a king.

Thus began the period in my life when from Monday to Friday I commuted from village to town, leaving home at 6.30

a.m. and returning at 6 p.m. I spent the evenings, weekends and national holidays testing out in practice in my rural laboratory the theories of rural development expounded by experts in the offices of government ministries.

The Green Revolution

This was the era of the great 'Green Revolution' and the American 'Hunger Project' which promised that all the hungry people of the world would be fed by the year 2000. Along with all my colleagues in the Ministry of Rural Development I was persuaded to believe that by using hybrid seeds and chemical fertilizers food crops could be made to yield up to six times the weight of grain previously grown by traditional farming methods.

I persuaded Daniel to plough with his oxen two acres of his four acre plot of land in Chipapa and I lent him money for hybrid seed and chemical fertilizer. We had good rains that year and every maize plant shot up to seven feet tall, each one with at least two cobs as thick as a man's wrist. No one in all the villages around had ever seen anything like it. They came and stood in wonder at the power of white man's magic (the name they gave to the white powder we sprinkled over the ground was 'musamu' meaning 'medicine').

Four hundred miles away in the North Western Province where I was running an agricultural project with British and Dutch volunteers they heard about Daniel's maize garden, and Chief Kasempa with his councillors came all the way by Landrover to witness this miracle.

Presidential visit to Chipapa

Word got through to the President in State House of the poor villager who had been hard pressed to feed his own family but now in one season had a crop that would give him enough

38

surplus maize for sale to pay off his loan and bury a wad of bank notes in a tin box in the mud floor of his house. There would be more than enough to supply all his family needs for over a year.

Parts of our road had been washed away in the heavy rains and though passable in my 'coffee pot' car were not negotiable by the presidential Mercedes Benz, so Kaunda, who wanted his whole government to know that the day of Zambia's prosperity had dawned, ordered two army helicopters to transport them to Chipapa.

We were given only three days to make frantic preparations for the presidential visit but really there was not much we could do but sweep up the rotting fruit and dead leaves beneath the great spreading fig tree down by the lake in preparation for the presidential indaba.

On the appointed day a despatch rider came with a message from State House to the headmaster of the school giving orders to the children to run into their classrooms when they saw the helicopters in the sky because the school football field had been chosen for the landing pad. When they arrived in a cloud of red dust we saw that Kaunda had been as good as his word. Not only had he brought the Ministers of Agriculture, Natural Resources, Rural Development and Local Government but also the Ministers of Education, Economic and Social Development, the Chief of Police, the Director of the Prison Services and the Commander of the Zambia National Youth Service.

Daniel led them proudly through his forest of towering maize stalks. They felt the weight and thickness of the cobs and wished the managers on their own private farms would do as well. At the indaba the President praised Daniel for all his hard work (quite forgetting Sarah and Janala who had done all the planting and weeding and spreading of the fertilizer). Knowing that his speech would be reported in full on local radio, he called on all village farmers to follow this poor man's example and by so doing eradicate the threat of hunger from the land.

The next year the people of Chipapa set up their own 'Productivity Council'. Each of the hundred members borrowed money from the Land Bank to purchase hybrid seed and fertilizer. Unfortunately the rains failed in mid season, the standing maize withered before producing any cobs and everyone ended up in debt.

The Women's Poultry Co-op

Meanwhile with help from the government poultry officer in Mazabuka, Sarah with thirteen other women started a poultry club. They worked in pairs, each couple agreeing to look after a little flock of broiler chickens and Emden geese and Khaki Campbell ducks, for one day in the week. Fortunately two women in the co-op were members of the Seventh Day Adventist church who worship on Saturdays, so they did their stint on Sundays when the others went to church.

None of the women nor I had any experience of looking after day old chicks but the man at the hatchery in Mazabuka showed us how to brood them in a box with a paraffin lantern to keep them warm at night. The baby chickens were no problem but we nearly lost the day old ducklings. All went well for the first three days but on the forth day, thinking they would enjoy it, we let them out when it was raining. They did love it but having no mother duck to teach them otherwise they rushed around with little beaks in the air to catch the heavy drops of rain and nearly drowned themselves. Just in time we rescued them and dried them out with the warm cuddle of our hands.

It was not long before we had a fleet of a hundred ducks cruising round the lake. They loved to dabble in the muddy margins of the dam gobbling up the water snails which harbour in their guts the dangerous bilharzia parasite. For the first time since the dam was made it was safe for the children to swim and splash in the water.

The Young Farmers' Club

A great part of my work in the Ministry of Rural Development was to try and persuade the government that it was a waste of time and money to settle urban youths as farmers in rural areas if the young men already living in the villages were failing to earn a decent living there. I knew that the best way to influence government policy would be by practical demonstration rather than argument. So I set about recruiting some of the young men in the village to start their own Young Farmers' Club. They wanted to have a regular monthly income rather than an annual income from a seasonal crop, so they decided to try growing vegetables for sale in Lusaka. I gave them all the assistance I could, even bringing out a young man from Britain to live and work with them and teach them the basic elements of organic horticulture.

However I had completely underestimated the social and economic forces with which they would have to contend and although we made a good beginning the project never took root. Out of the ten young men who started the club only one remained after two years and he ended up working for a European farmer who grew flowers for export by air to Britain. By village standards he earned good money but being illiterate he could not read the 'poison' label on the can of insecticide used to spray his master's roses. Not realising that the liquid should never be used on food crops he took some home with him one day to kill the corn crickets on his maize cobs. Six months later he and his wife and two of their children died after eating an evening meal made from the flour which she had

41

pounded from their own poisoned cobs.

I did not keep a diary during the years I worked first in the Zambia Youth Service and then in the Land Resettlement division of the Ministry of Rural Development but when I returned from leave in September 1969 I decided to do so . It is from that diary I have made the extracts which now carry the Chipapa story forward to 1974 when I finally returned to Britain.

CHAPTER 4
Chipapa Diary 1969-1974

September 18th 1969 The Church and the land

Yesterday I arrived back in Lusaka from short leave. There is bad news from Chipapa. Last night Janala, Daniel's married daughter was waiting by the roadside for a lift when she was assaulted, robbed and left badly cut and bruised with two bones broken in her leg. It happened in broad daylight, but there were no witnesses and the police have no clues. I must get back to the village as soon as I can.

Late in the morning the Moderator of the United Church of Zambia and our local Kafue minister dropped in to see me about the problems caused by squatters moving onto the land at Kafue Mission. A number of attempts have been made to develop the land for farming, but they have not been successful. The Church now finds itself with a big Secondary School giving a high level of academic education, training boys for the 'O' level examination, and a large tract of undeveloped, agriculturally marginal land onto which 'squatters' have begun to move. The Church knows what it would like to do, which is either to give the Secondary School an agricultural bias, getting the boys to grow their own food and so hopefully gain an interest in farming, or else to encourage settlement by young men trained at the Chipembi farm institute, to grow crops for the rapidly expanding industrial population of Kafue Town seven miles away. But knowing what it ought to do, and doing it are worlds apart. The Church has neither the capital nor the managerial capacity to develop its own land. Until now we have been able to put off the problem, and settle with our conscience by promising ourselves that next year we will do something about it, next year when we are a little less hard pressed for money, or staff, or time to do the thousand other things we want to do. But now we cannot put it off any longer because since the referendum on land last June it becomes clear that our Government is going to say that the land shall belong to those who use it and not to those who long ago were lucky enough to have the money to buy it cheap. Sometimes the Church in the past has toyed with the idea of selling some of its land, but there has always been someone to suggest that if we would hang on a little longer the price might go up.

The Moderator enquired if I knew of anyone qualified to run a farm scheme at the Mission because he knows that I have been in England recruiting agriculturalists to come to Zambia to help us in the development of our rural areas. I am quite clear in my own mind what ought to be done, but I have no confidence that the United Church of Zambia, as presently organised, has the will power to act creatively in a situation like this. There is hardly a secondary school in Zambia taking the issue seriously of how to give young men a vocation for the land, but Kafue could do it. All it needs is a good practical farmer to come from overseas to spend three years settling five young Secondary School leavers on five acres each just near the school. The present generation of school boys at Kafue must be able to see with their own eyes some of their peers earning a decent living from the land. Only then will they believe. The capital required for establishing each settler must be kept small, otherwise the project has no relevance for the great mass of jobless school leavers who have no other future but a life on the land. Our attempts to settle young men from the Zambia Youth Service on the land has at least driven home that lesson.

As for all the other land, I think the Moderator was faintly surprised to hear me suggest that there might be an alternative use for this valuable riverside asset. After all there is plenty of agricultural potential around Kafue town for feeding the population there, but there is only one Kafue river bank where the newly urbanised population can come at weekends to watch hippos and lily-trotters, to hear the song of robin chats and the call of fish eagles, to see the startling colours of malachite kingfishers and the Knysna louris which live in the tall trees by the river. Zambia spends thousands of kwachas to develop great game parks for American tourists, but hardly a penny for the recreation of the workers in the chemical factory and the cotton mill at nearby Kafue. For once let the church stop asking how it can cash in on its inherited wealth and regain the freedom to sing honestly about "all things bright and beautiful".

This evening I went out to Chipapa. Men have been working on the road, filling up the pot-holes and the gullies with gravel, but no trenches have been dug to take off the storm water, so when the rain comes next month it will all wash out again. The ducks and turkeys have grown marvellously, and we have a lot more Emden geese from Mazabuka. The Harco layers are a disappointment, too finely bred I fear for the harsh conditions of the village. The warm welcome I was given by Sarah, Daniel, Chipo and the others has helped greatly to thaw an aching heart still frozen up by leaving my family in England.

September 19th Dr Fritz Schumacher visits our Village. Is the drift to the towns unstoppable?

Dr Schumacher of the Intermediate Technology Development Group is here from England on a special assignment for Kenneth Kaunda. I have never met him before, but whenever I have read reports of the lectures he has given on economic development, it has set all my glory bells ringing, and his report on Tanzania last year was a masterpiece of clarity and

45

understanding. I have always been intrigued by the fact that Schumacher, who is the British Coal Board's economic consultant, should not only concern himself with African problems, but have such a sure insight into them and some practical ideas for their solution. I was afraid he might spend all his time in Zambia meeting Government officials at top level and being taken round our show pieces of development, so I invited him to come down to Chipapa for a meal. I took him on the regular Chipapa public tour. We looked at the ducks and the geese, and I explained how we are trying to build up our flock of Aylesburys because they are better mothers than the Khaki Campbells, and what we want is meat production because the marketing of duck eggs is such a problem. I showed him our experiments with intermediate technology pumps. We had a look at the Boys Club's sad little garden and old Shachifwa's dying village. We went into the village shop to record the high price of a tin of pilchards and a packet of Surf. But I could see that he was not thinking about the minutiae of our village technology, he was leaving that to his secretary Mrs Porter. He was seeing the people in their poverty and wondering how they can live like that. We went back to the house and Sarah cooked us some rice and stewed duck, unfortunately it had not stewed long enough and was rather tough. I don't think he found it very easy talking to me because his Coal Board world seems hardly at any point to touch my peasant world of Chipapa. I was glad to have Dr. Krapf (German theologian and Presidential Advisor on Social Policy) along to be a kind of interpreter of ideas. There was no language problem, it was rather a philosophical one. I was delighted to find that Schumacher does not regard 'Intermediate Technology' as a kind of cause under whose banner we all must march if we are to win the war against poverty, ignorance and disease. He does not try to see it as the

46

means by which we can stem the drift of young men to the towns and for creating some idyllic kind of rural community life. He has the courage to question everything, not least our belief in the long haul, the hard slog and agony of step by step rural development.

"Suppose" he says, "there is some sediment of truth in what people are saying, that nothing, but nothing, is going to stop the drift to the towns, that after all there is no technological difficulty in accommodating all Zambia's five million people in three or four major population centres along the line of rail and on the Copperbelt. Could people really be any worse off in urban poverty than they now are in their rural poverty? Why not lash out our money on tractors and other labour saving machines, which if people were not living in thousands of scattered villages, but in close communities, might in the end prove economic?"

Schumacher was putting up an Aunt Sally to see us knock it down, but he knows as well as we do the almost demonic power of the copper mines which not only dominate our entire economy but which super-charge the winds of change and suck us inexorably into their de-humanising vortex. Schumacher knows that unless we find a successful means of developing the rural areas within the period of our next five year plan, nothing can save them. They will become a waste land abandoned by the young where the old are left alone to die.

We were five in the tiny front room of our house, so the ten members of the Boys' club who had joined us for supper had to sit outside. It made me uncomfortable that we could not all be together, and I know I must extend my little house with a roof made big enough to include us all. There was a brilliant moon when I went out to talk with the boys and I knew as I spoke with them that I must not spend too much of my time living for the day when everyone in Chipapa has piped water to his house, when there is a fixed price for turkey meat, and a sure market for all our eggs, and when the fields grow soya beans as well as maize. My real job is to find a way to free Godfrey, Nathan, Zunda, Leonard and all the other young men who grow up now in Chipapa from their own Utopian dreams. It may be that their children will one day operate computers in Lusaka or plough the fields by remote controlled tractors. I do not know and it is not worth spending a great deal of time trying to find out. The boys have only one life in the here and now of Chipapa and they must come to terms with it, and live it to the full, and if intermediate technology is going to help them, then we will use it. Whether these boys ever become rich and successful farmers is irrelevant; that they be free to take hold of life with both hands and enjoy living it is supremely important.

September 20th Duck Eggs and Sarah's dream

After supper this evening Sarah Kalambalala came in for a chat. Daniel her husband left early this morning for a church meeting at Kafue Mission to discuss arrangements for the Jubilee celebrations commemorating fifty years of missionary work in this area. I wish he would spent the time building his chicken house. He will never have it ready when the rains come.

Sarah, who is the mainstay of the Chipapa Women's Poultry Co-operative, told us of her concern about the Harco layers. From ninety five birds we got only twenty one eggs today. There were three dozen eggs from the Khaki Campbells, but the village people will not buy duck eggs. Somehow they have caught hold of our European prejudice against duck eggs, which is pure blind prejudice, because they are just as nutritious and no more harmful than hens' eggs, but that is the thing about prejudice, once it is there it is very hard to shift. I wish I knew why the hens do not lay. Naturally I put it down to something wrong in the management, but the experts say it is probably poor stock. All I want is for the egg production to go up so that the Women's Co-op stops losing money, but I am not a poultry expert so I can't argue. Sarah also wanted to explain that when there is some profit she does not want it distributed at the end of the month because the women fritter it away. It would be better to let the money accumulate for six months because then it would seem more and could be used for buying a dress or paying for a child's school uniform. How much we need to get a thrift society started in the village, but what an uphill task it is going to be.

Sarah began to tell me about a dream she had last night which woke her up and which has been worrying her ever since. I usually feel terribly embarrassed when people tell me their dreams because I know they want me to interpret them, and that makes me feel such a fraud, but Sarah was obviously troubled and wanted to talk to someone so I let her tell me. It was quite short and simple.

She had seen two aeroplanes fly over Chipapa from east to west. The first was full of African people and it flew over the hill and landed and all the people got out and walked to the village. The second plane had in it a man all dressed in white. He was sitting down and she could not see his face, but when he was directly overhead, she saw floating down from the sky a cob of maize, very white, as white as finely pounded maize flour, and with the maize cob were three shelled ground nuts. She received these into her hands and found suddenly all the other passengers from the other plane gathered round her and they were praying.

That was all. I asked her if she had often had this dream, but she said it was the first time, though right at the end of the dream they were all together in a great house, and she had sometimes dreamt about the same house before, and it was filled then with seats all covered in gold. I asked if she had heard anyone speak in her dream. Had she received any message? But she hadn't.

What was I to do? I have very vivid dreams myself and get a lot of fun from remembering them, even the nightmares. But for Sarah it is different. Her dream has significance. She must try to understand what it means. There are no old men left in the village whom she respects enough to go to for help, so she has turned to me. I cannot leave her alone with it, so I said I would think and pray about it and we shall together try to understand what it could mean. It is a big responsibility to interpret other people's dreams, but not one I as a Christian minister can duck.

It is strangely quiet for a moonlit Saturday night. No drums are beating and no-one seems to be having a beer drink or a dance tonight.

September 21st Farmers still deep in debt - more chemicals and tractors not the answer

It has been a quiet Chipapa Sunday for me with forty people in church and the preacher speaking on the parable of the sower.

This afternoon Daniel came in with some money from those members of our 'Chipapa Productivity Council' who had sold their grain after harvest. They are still all heavily in debt after the crop failure of the 1967/68 drought. They had borrowed money again in 1968/69 for the purchase of good seed and fertilizer hoping to get enough surplus on their food crop to sell it and pay off both their debts, but the heaviest rains for ten years swamped the crops and there was again hardly any surplus for sale after putting aside enough grain for themselves and their poultry for the coming months. We all know that the provision of seasonal credit is vital for the peasants if they are to get seed and fertilizer for the improvement of crops, but when through no fault of their own they are hit two seasons running by bad weather, it is hard for them to believe that borrowing money to improve the crop is really worth while. In the past they have ploughed and planted when the rains come and if they have been lucky they have had enough food to eat and a little left over for sale. If they have been unlucky, they have tightened their belts and got through the hunger months by digging roots in the bush. But that was all before they became so dependent on a cash economy. For a man so much in debt, Daniel was still hopeful. Perhaps the good Lord would give him a good season this coming year and somehow he will scrape together enough money to pay his debt, but there are some members of our Productivity Council who do not have even enough maize in their grain bins to see them through to the next harvest and they can pay back nothing so they go deeper and deeper into debt. A great part of our problem at Chipapa is our dependence on maize. This is why our experiments this year with soya beans and vegetables and the management of livestock are so important. The conservation of the poultry manure would save us a lot of expenditure on chemical fertilizers. The introduction of better seed alone will double the crop, but that would not help to get across the fundamental lesson that we must not take out of the ground more than we put into it.

This is a hard lesson for us to learn who live in Zambia, where for a thousand years the people have had enough land to settle on where they wished, to chop down trees and burn them and plant their crops and move on to new ground when after three or four years the old became exhausted. It was not a dangerous way of living when land was limitless and the bush had time to regenerate and return fertility to the soil, but those

51

days have gone. Now there is pressure on the land because the hoe, the plough, and the tractor have enabled people to cultivate much larger acreages. Not only is the land exhausted but time is running out too. It is now too late for an easy slow transition from the old methods to the new. There must be an agricultural revolution or we shall destroy the land as the Tonga are doing in the Gwembe valley. I disagree profoundly with those who believe that the revolution can be achieved by the sudden introduction of mechanised agriculture, hybrid seed and artificial fertilizers. It is not that Africans cannot be taught to handle machines and manage farms. Of course they can, as one day they will work and manage the copper mines. The real revolution has got to come in the minds of the peasants themselves, an understanding that the soil is a living thing which needs not 'medicine' (our local name for fertilizer), but what the doctors call 'T.L.C.' - tender loving care. But if ever I talk like this here in the Department of Agriculture of our Ministry, I am given my dunce's cap and put in the corner with all the other cranky members of the 'muck and mystery' school.

September 22nd Men on the Moon - Tractors

I was having my duck egg for breakfast this morning when Chipapa's Headman old Shachifwa, Daniel's father, came in. It was the first time that I had seen him since getting back because he has been over at Chipongwe trying to run a butchery. He must be nearly eighty now, because he paid his first poll tax in 1910. It is one of the things I like about our house at Chipapa, that people drop in unexpectedly for a meal. He asked me what I thought about the Americans having flown to the moon. He said he believed it because he knew that the Americans were very clever people, but there had been a great deal of discussion in the village amongst the older people who found it impossible to believe. They had two difficulties. One was that people could not walk on the moon because they would not have any sky there since they were in the sky already. The other problem was about God. God is somewhere up there in the sky because he sends rain, and nothing in the lives of the people is more important than rain. Somehow, men on the moon would interfere with God's benevolence.

"Anyway" Shachifwa said "what's the point of going there since they found no trees to build houses with, and no grass for grazing cattle."

The newspaper today has a front page spread about the 'lazy and dishonest farmers' who borrow money from the Government and do not pay it back. I suppose they think that Shachifwa is one of them. In 1966 he was persuaded by an enthusiastic Credit Officer to borrow £100 with which to hire tractors. He was told that the oxen he had relied on in the past were far too slow to get the land all ploughed at the first rains. That season was the good one when Daniel grew his 'miracle crop' using good seed and fertilizer, but after Shachifwa's land had been tractor ploughed he planted his usual poor seed and put on no 'medicine'. The result was that in spite of the large acreage his crop was poor and he has paid nothing off his loan.

September 24th A bush fire

I had to give a lecture on rural development at the National Institute of Public Administration at 5.00 o'clock. We had a very good discussion afterwards, and by the time I had picked up the people who had come in to see Janala, it was nearly 8.00 o'clock when we got back to Chipapa. As we approached the house I saw a forest fire burning on the hill. Daniel was away and Sarah had to get supper for Chipo and Trevor, so I went out alone with the two dogs to beat it out. Fortunately the fire was backing up against the wind and I managed to get it under control before it crept over the brow of the hill, but I had exhausted nearly all my strength by the time the job was done.

October 3rd Potatoes at tuppence a pound

I bought some dried fish for the boys and headed back to Chipapa. I was tired after a long hot day - we had the hottest September for seventeen years. Only three members of the Boys' Club turned up for our weekly meeting. I began to question them very closely about this and discovered that most of them have lost heart. We have reaped a fairly good potato crop, but the maximum we can get from the Marketing Board in Lusaka is 2p per pound, while the same potatoes are being sold on the streets for 5p. I can hardly blame the boys for saying that the return they get for their labour is so small that it is not worth the effort and there can be no future for them in small scale farming. They see the men who are working on the road and getting 50p per day. I am told that all the club members who come from Mulendema spend their days in Peter Mbewe's Tavern. When I asked where they get the money from for the beer, I was told that they wait for people coming out of town who treat them at the bar.

We are having a problem getting water onto the garden because a grass fire burnt out a section of the plastic piping to the dam and also destroyed a number of our tomato plants.

October 5th Do we sack drunkards?

Sunday mornings before church is our time for getting the house tidy. We are a bit cramped just now because the chicken room and grain store is not ready. Matthew Ndunda and another local farmer Juda Kibika gave us a thousand bricks each, but we have been building for six months and still the roof is not on. The result is that my bedroom which is 8ft by 8ft has to be used to store the eggs and the potatoes. Anyway it is better than the rainy season when I had to brood the day old chicks by my bedside. Their cheeping would wake me up if the hurricane lamp went out.

In church this morning we were six men, seven women and five children. Daniel preached from John chapter 15 about The True Vine. We had a discussion after the sermon about casting away the branches of the vine which bear no fruit and pruning those which do bear fruit. We applied it to the Boys' Club, and asked ourselves whether we ought to throw out the boys who get drunk at the tavern. There was also the problem of Lydia in the poultry co-op who is always letting us down.

October 8th Whiteman's magic

Old Man Shachifwa came with me to Lusaka this morning. He always points to me the house of a certain man which we pass on the way into Lusaka. He was notorious for his rough handling of 'the natives' and once killed a workman with his bare hands. The Old Man asked me where the Europeans got their 'medicine' from. He often talks about the European's 'mano' which includes power, skill, cleverness, wisdom. Do they get it as Africans do from the bark of trees and roots? Or do they dig it out of the ground? We passed a tractor on the road and the Old Man said,

"Ah, that is what makes the European farmers rich, if only I had a tractor, just to get the maize planted when the rains come, I would be rich too."

He is old and his houses are tumbling down. He is always asking how he can get the money to buy some sheets of corrugated iron because he knows he soon will not have the strength to cut poles and grass for thatching.

October 10th In the darkness a candle burns

It has been a hot and messy day with at the end of it nothing accomplished. I felt disappointment and depression seeping into every corner of my being and the more I bailed out the more it rose, and by evening I was ready to sink. I slept through the eight o'clock news then went straight to bed. I was wakened in the small hours by the geese, but the dogs were not barking so I did not go out to investigate. I lit the candle and lay fighting the depression of the previous day. Perhaps it was the candle flame in the darkness of the room that made me think of the light that overcomes the darkness in the world. Something set me thinking about the parables of the Kingdom, the seed that grows secretly, the pearl that makes it worth while to sell everything else to get it, and the kingdom is not something far away that is for my grandchildren's children and Kaunda's grandchildren and Chipo to enter. It is here, and it is only my fault if I do not go in. I waste far too much time prising open all the wrong doors. Let's face it, the door is an open door and children can go through, no trouble at all.

October 11th A dying Ox and a child with Kwashiokor

Janala has been discharged from hospital today so I went to Lusaka to fetch her. Her leg is still in plaster but she can walk with crutches.

I picked up the two policemen who guard the Chipapa's grain store at night. For some reason the Police Station at Chilanga had not sent transport to collect them. One of them had been at school in Uganda. He thought it was a wonderful country where the cost of living was very much lower than Zambia. There you can buy all the bananas you can eat for 6d whereas here you can sometimes pay 6d for one single banana.

"Everyone in Uganda is well educated," he said "even the

loafers in Kampala have been to secondary school!"

When I got back to Chipapa at midday, I found five of the boys sweating away trying to water the garden with buckets carried from the well. They were not using the pump which sucks water from the dam because the fire had burnt out a section of the black plastic piping. They were waiting for a chance to go to Lusaka to get another section of piping. I quickly realised that all they needed to do was to move the pump nearer to the water and re-arrange the reticulation in the garden. It only took an hour to get it fixed up. The black piping was so hot in the sun that we had to take our shirts off to make oven cloths to hold it. What a revolution this plastic piping has made to our problems of water reticulation. A completely unskilled person like myself can do in a matter of hours what before it used to take a skilled plumber days of work, cutting and threading and joining galvanized pipes.

In the evening I walked along the edge of our 'little lake' enjoying the sight of geese grazing on the bank and our flotilla of noisy ducks on the water. A boy came driving what looked like a fine healthy looking ox, but it was actually very sick because every now and again it would stumble and almost fall to the ground. There was something wrong with its hind quarters, but I could see no lesion in the flesh. The boy said it would soon die. It is one of Kapipe's four oxen, and that will make it tough for him when we start ploughing next month.

There were women and children fishing with canes along the lake shore. They seem only to catch little ones and are lucky if they have a small plate full at the end of the day. One of the women who comes from Taulo's place on the other side had three of her little daughters standing in the water with their fishing canes. How thankful I am that our ducks by gobbling up the snails have eradicated all danger of them being infected with bilharzia. She had another toddler and a year old baby on the bank. The baby's hair was dusty red and I would think showing all the signs of malnutrition. I tried to explain that the child was not being properly fed, but all the woman could do was come out of the water and give it her shrivelled breast. As I talked to her wondering what I could do, I was thinking of the boy I had picked up that morning who spends £8 a month on his beer.

October 24th A snake in the thatch

I started at dawn to day to get a new roof put on my house at Chipapa, but first I had to clear the house of everything before we stripped off the thatch and all the rotten purlins. I had a lot of helpers, Daniel and Jackson from the village, and Leonard and Nathan from the Boys' Club.

Leonard got a fright when a small green snake came out of the thatch and wrapped itself round his neck, he pulled it away before it bit him which was lucky, since I think it was a deadly boomslang. It was one of the hottest days I have known, working up for rain and we had to keep asking for cups of water to be handed up to us on the roof. By dusk the last nail had been hammered home, the new veranda had been added and asbestos sheets had taken the place of bundles of grass, but only just in time, for it began to pour with rain.

October 25th We put a new roof on the house

I went over early this morning to Jackson's house to see if he would help me with the alterations to the house, because he is about the only person in the village who knows how to use a level and lay bricks, but he was busy using the grass I had taken off my roof to thatch his grain bin. He obviously had to get his food store covered before another storm came, so there was nothing for it but to teach Nathan how to lay bricks, and even Chipo, aged eight, helped me knock down an inner wall and shovel out the rubble. Daniel was busy gathering firewood for his brick kiln, so Nathan started on the whitewash.

At about midday Godfrey, Daniel's nephew and a member of the Boys' Club, wandered over to get some medicine for a bee sting. I heard an argument begin between him and Daniel. They have always had a fairly strong antipathy to each other. Daniel thinks Godfrey is a loafer and does his best every time they meet to persuade Godfrey that he ought to be a good boy and work hard and come to church. Godfrey thinks Daniel is an interfering old so-and-so. The argument about whether Godfrey should or should not have been helping us with the house went on and on and they shouted louder and louder until Daniel was saying,

"Get out of my sight you lazy good-for-nothing ..."

and Godfrey was saying,

"I'm not going 'till I get back my membership ticket of the Boys' Club, because I have resigned from now on, you ..."

Then they began to fight. Daniel is a little man, but he is very tough and when I heard Godfrey howling in pain I had to go and separate them before any serious damage was done. Nathan went on quietly with his building and Leonard with his whitewashing. It was a village scene they were all too familiar with and their only comment was,

"If I had been Godfrey I would have run a bit faster to get out of Daniel's way."

I think Daniel was a bit ashamed of what he had done because he came and worked with me 'till dusk, hammering out a piece of old zinc to made a gutter for the roof.

November 3rd Is all overseas aid bad?

Daniel came with me to town this morning and I left him at the mortuary where people were gathering round the body of Herbert Shankwaya who was killed in a motor car accident on

Saturday. Daniel spent most of yesterday helping to dig the grave of a woman who died in Shincebe's village which is just over on the other side of the dam. Last Wednesday he attended Chief Nkomesha's funeral. This preoccupation with the disposal of the dead is enormously time consuming. The bigger a man's extended family and the wider the circle of his friends, the more time he must spend paying respect to the dead. I wonder how they deal with the funeral problem in communist China. I am sure that funerals used to play a very big part in the life of the old China but it certainly reduces the number of man hours that can go into food production in the rural areas.

Bob Liebentall, the young economist who works down the corridor from my office in Lusaka, came in for a chat this afternoon. He has been very busy over the past few weeks working out the details of an enormous nation-wide cattle scheme being sponsored by the World Bank. Bob was at Oxford under Sutcliffe and he wrote his thesis on the subject of 'Aid to Under Developed Countries'. He believes on the whole that all aid is totally bad because of its effect on the recipient. In theory when the World Bank steps in with a massive loan to put our cattle industry on its economic feet, we should in Zambia be saving money which would go into another development project which we would not have been able to undertake had it not been for the World Bank loan. What happens of course is that we take the loan, hope we shall be able to pay the interest on it when the time comes and immediately spend what we have 'saved' on increasing our consumption. It wouldn't matter if we spent it on more capital goods for real development, but we buy more Mercedes Benz for more Ministers to ride around in. All too often aid is 'money given by the poor in rich countries to help the rich in poor countries'.

Not being an economist myself I cannot really argue with

Bob and I know that he is more right than wrong and that Nyerere's economic policy in Tanzania is a great deal sounder than Kaunda's in Zambia, but this total dismissal of all 'aid', however it is given, as a bad thing for Africa smacks to me of the argument that wine is bad because people get drunk and sex is wrong because people have too many babies. I cannot believe that it is totally a mistake for the rich to help the poor. Giving and receiving must somehow be conceived as a complementary thing. We have to work this thing out in Chipapa between myself as a rich man and Daniel the poor man before we have any advice to give to Oxfam, or Christian Aid, or the British Government, or Kaunda, or the boys in our Boys' Club, or in the Zambia Youth Service. Jesus did say that it is more blessed to give than to receive, so there must be a right way of giving and he did tell the rich young ruler to give away all that he had to the poor. That might be the secret of course. It could be that the only kind of giving by the rich that is any good is when they give everything. Perhaps 1% of the G.N.P. of rich countries is quite literally worse than nothing because it is 'the all' that they can spare and that is not 'the all' that Jesus was talking about. What is 'the all' that I have got to give to Chipapa?

November 5th We must return to the land or we shall starve

I have come to the conclusion, as I did when I was trying to persuade people ten years ago to accept the inevitability of African majority rule, that when people's minds are closed, no amount of talk will open them. I can argue the case for the hoe and the ox over against the tractor at this stage of development until I am blue in the face, but I have never yet got a 'mechanisation' man to change his mind because of my arguments. What we need is a real crisis in Zambia, economic or political, which will close the door to the import of tractors, mechanical cotton pickers, luxury cheeses and Mercedes Benz and make us recognise that we either return to the land or starve.

Fortunately I feel no responsibility to engineer such a crisis because it will come as certainly as night follows day. I think the financial and the political crises will coincide.

Tonight I read Colin Morris's book, 'Unyoung, Uncoloured and Unpoor'. This is the book that will make his name and for which he will be remembered. He has faced the crucial issue of our time and said as no one else can ever say again, the prophetic word. I have now got to try and apply what Colin says - not in terms of the struggle between Kaunda and Smith, but between the peasants in Zambia and the Ba-Mercedes-Benz, between the rural poor and the urban rich. It is a terrifying thought that violence may be the only way of righting wrong. We have however an inescapable responsibility to exhaust every other means of bringing about a change before we resort to violence. I believe the end of the road has been reached as far as Rhodesia is concerned. Ian Smith is as representative of evil as Hitler was and he should be tried for murder but this is not the time for violence in Zambia.

November 6th We sugar the pill, but they will not swallow it

This morning I drove from the Copperbelt to Lusaka thinking all the time of Colin's book. The Jesus of history now seems much more real. The probability that the Cross was the badge of death for the Zealots does not make a lot of sense to me but the better we understand the Jesus of history, the more relevant he becomes for our day. If we could find a way of smuggling thousands of copies of Colin's book into Rhodesia we might get the Church there to consider the possibility of becoming the spearhead of the movement of national liberation.

This afternoon I met with officials of our Ministry and the

United Nations team to consider their preliminary report on the Zambia Youth Service. It became quite clear as we talked that the situation has gone beyond the stage when it can be patched up. There must be a quite new approach of the ZYS leaders to the problems of settling youth on the land. We made polite suggestions about the need for a co-ordinating committee to relate the training programme of the ZYS to that of the Department of Agriculture. We went once again over well trodden ground explaining why co-operative settlements have been a failure and we tried to sugar the pill for the Youth Service by explaining how their youth settlements were only a part of a much bigger question, but their minds are closed. For them there are but two alternatives. Either youths must go back into a primitive past, when naked savages cultivated their 'slash-and-burn' gardens with their digging sticks, or they must make the great leap forward into modernity when the farmer dons blue overalls on a weekday and rides his tractor, while on Sunday he drives to church or the local beer garden in his Mercedes Benz. There are no intermediate stages, there is just the old and the new, the past and the future, the darkness and the light. They will not stand steadfastly in the present, proud of their own past and humbly asking questions of the future.

November 13th George Mwando's ox killed by a hyena

This morning I was listening to the BBC outline of the British Press comment on the world news when Daniel Kalambalala came in for a chat. His preoccupation with funerals over the last month has as usual made him fall far behind in his farming schedule. November 15th is the recommended date for the last planting of the maize crop, as the best results from maize are obtained when the plant grows during the warm days of November and December and the cobs can fatten in the early weeks of the New Year. The yield drops rapidly as the date of planting is delayed but Daniel has not yet started looking for his oxen which have strayed off somewhere in the hills towards the Kafue River. He is still busy trying to get the thatch put on the roof of his chicken house before the heavy rains wash away the mud brick walls. Last night a hyena killed one of George Mwando's four oxen less than half a mile from our house and a young steer drowned itself in the little stream which came down in flood yesterday afternoon. In the whole village I have seen only one man ploughing. They all know the value of early planting but 'buzuba leta tunji' - 'tomorrow is another day'.

Procrastination is not the same as 'taking no care for the morrow'. Procrastination is what you do when you have given up hope that anything can ever change. That is the basic attitude of the people in Chipapa. Anyway Kapipe is going off today to look for the lost cattle in the hills and tomorrow Daniel's brother-in-law is coming to help with the thatching of the chicken house. I picked up the man who used to work for us as a garden boy in Lusaka and now lives in Chipapa. He asked for a lift into town to buy a bag of hybrid maize seed. It will cost him £7.50 for a hundred pounds which will be enough to plant five acres. I feel I ought not to be going to Nairobi for the Youth Conference on Saturday, but should be here to help the people in Chipapa get on with the planting. No one is coming to buy the chicks that the women have been brooding and which are now inoculated against fowl pest and ready to go out to the people. It is partly our fault because we never got started on the poultry evangelism campaign in the surrounding villages. We also procrastinate.

December 2nd How blessed are the poor?
This morning I was standing by the car waiting for Sarah to

bring a basket of grain which she had already asked me to take up to Annie Musunsa in town, and suddenly I was aware of the beauty of the day. Five egrets appeared high above the little lake, their wings brilliant white against a dark cloud and all the leaves of the trees had been washed by the rain in the night, and the low light of the sun shone on little Trevor's bright eyes and burnished the blackness of his skin.

I had been listening last night to a talk on the wireless about what man is doing to pollute the atmosphere of our world and contaminate the water of our rivers and lakes. The man who was lecturing said,

"Perhaps we should not be saying that there are too many 'undeveloped' countries in the world, but that there are too many 'developed' countries. It is the 'developed' countries with their factories and their machines which are the destroyers..."

I wonder if he is right? Could it be that encouraging the people who work the land above our lake to use artificial fertilizers in their fields, we might so increase the phosphate and nitrogen content of the water that one day the fish would die? Why did Sarah have to run after Trevor to catch him before he could get down to the lake and dress him up in his little shorts and shirt to take him to town?

"Behold the lilies of the field, they toil not, neither do they spin - yet Solomon in all his glory was not arrayed like one of those".

If the 'poor' are blessed and the rich are accursed then why do we spend so much of our effort on 'development' which in Western terms is trying to make poor people rich? I think there must be a great fallacy at the bottom of all our talk about 'World Development'. I have just been reading D. G. Arnott's review of Lester Pearson's report 'Partners in Development' and it appears that the one criterion of development is whether the annual economic growth rate of a poor country can be maintained at 6%. Zambias' growth rate is better than 6% but over the weekend seventeen people were killed outright in Lusaka alone in motor car accidents.

The copper mines can get richer and richer and we can export more and more copper and import more and more Mercedes Benz and when Robert McNamara at the World Bank looks at the statistics he can pat us on the head and tell us to go to the top of the class, but Chipo will be a year older and the chance of him finding a job when he leaves school is that much slimmer. Surely instead of the economists rating the poor on their G.N.P. they should now start assessing development in terms of the D.C.W. 'Distribution of the Common Wealth'.

Every year a nation produces wealth by the labour of its people and some way needs to be found for assessing the extent to which that wealth - whether it be copper bars or cabbages, is shared by everyone. The copper miner who works an eight-hour shift lashing ore underground on the Roan mine has no right to a higher wage than Daniel working for eight hours under the sun at Chipapa. But the problem is that Daniel doesn't - he digs graves and preaches at funerals and Kapipe spends most of the week getting drunk.

Who was Jesus talking about when he said 'blessed are ye poor'? It must have been the ordinary peasant folk in the villages of Gallilee. They were not unemployed nor were they starving under-nourished children. Who were the 'rich' whom he cursed? They must have been landowners and merchants and money lenders who had grown rich at the expense of others who worked for them.

CHAPTER 5

August 1970. Furrow Through The Hills

One day I decided to go with my friends to visit Shantumbu, an area which lies five miles due north of Chipapa. There was no proper road, really nothing more than an eroded cattle track through the trees. At one point after negotiating a narrow defile through the rocks, we climbed steeply out of a river bed, and there before my eyes was one of the most lovely sights I have ever seen in Zambia. In August the Central Province landscape is dusty and dry. The colours of the bush were russet brown, black and yellow, tawny like a lion's mane. The trees were bare of leaves, the grass fires had exposed the blackened rocks, but what I suddenly saw was a little green valley set there in the hills like an emerald dropped by chance from some jewel box in heaven.

As we drew near I saw women and children at work in the fields. There were long straight lines of curly lettuces, and Chinese cabbage, and tomatoes and onions and here and there big clumps of green banana trees. There must have been four or five acres under cultivation. There was water, but I could not see where it was coming from. There was no sound of diesel engines, no evidence of overhead electric cables bringing power to silently running pumps, no river or stream in the valley bottom, yet there it was, a richly watered oasis in the middle of nowhere with people growing the precious fruit and vegetables which everyone in Lusaka is crying out for.

We walked down through the gardens to greet the women, and I noticed how expertly the irrigation channels had been laid, how neatly the rows of crops had been arranged, and how free from weeds the whole garden seemed to be. A little runnel of clear water was flowing through the lettuces, and I assumed it must be coming from some hidden spring away up on the hillside, but I was wrong. The truth about the little stream in the bottom of the dry valley is stranger than any Zambian fiction.

On a farm outside Lusaka, where an old Dutchman had developed a little irrigation system, a semi-literate labourer called Filipo had learned one of the fundamental principles of hydrodynamics, which is simply that if you can keep water running downhill at a gradient just a little steeper than the contour, you can take it anywhere you like. About the year 1965, the Dutchman returned to his native land and Filipo came to settle with his wife and family, and his brothers and their families in this desolate place. They are members of Watchtower (Jehovah's Witnesses), and they wanted to get away from the UNIP people who had been bullying them. The only way they could find water in the dry season was to climb the steep hillside on the east side of their valley, and scramble down into a deep cleft of the hills where one of the perennial streams that trickle out of the escarpment flows down into the river below. Filipo traced the stream to its source and found that he was looking down on the other side of the hill from his own valley. He then got the crazy idea that if he could divert the stream from its own valley into his valley, he could have running water for his crops. With his brother he started work with hoe and pick-axe and shovel to lead the water where he wanted it to go. Winding in and out amongst the boulders, under the roots of trees, through gravel and stone, they laboriously hacked and shovelled and dug their way. At one point in order to cross a small ravine, they had to make an aqueduct from corrugated iron sheets supported on bush poles. After working for months on end, they finally brought the waters of the little stream down into their valley, and started to make their garden.

Soon they were producing more vegetables than they could

haul to Lusaka on their bicycles. They decided that they needed a small truck, but they knew that even if they could get the money to buy one, it would be of no use to them unless they could drive it up through the Shantumbu escarpment, where there was only a narrow cycle track. Again they took to their picks and shovels and made a mile-long road out to the top of the valley. There is one quick way of making money in Zambia and that is by cutting trees and burning clamps of charcoal to sell in the town. This the two brothers did, and before long they had enough money to buy a little truck.

I suppose if Filipo had been a well educated man, and had known how to write up a project for the Technical Planning committee of the Land Use Division of the Ministry of Rural Development, he might before he started have applied for a loan from the Government for his vegetable production scheme. I can just imagine the chairman of the committee introducing the subject at the monthly meeting of his experts.

"Gentlemen, we have a request for assistance from a man who wants to grow vegetables in the Shantumbu area. We have made a preliminary investigation of the project from our aerial photographs. You will see if you look at the maps in front of you that it is intended to take water in a furrow from A to B. Quite a bit of blasting will be required. There is no road into the area so we shall have to use a helicopter to fly in the equipment. I have asked our agricultural economist to do a feasibility study of the marketing angle and of course a cost benefit analysis, but it is obvious we shall have to turn down this request purely on economic grounds because of course the government would never recoup the capital outlay - not in a hundred years".

I know of course that the number of Filipos in Zambia is few and far between. I know that in too many Zambian villages the people booze away the day, and spend the night in drunken stupor. I know that we still must have experts from overseas to help us build the dams we need. But somewhere along the line since we achieved our Independence the link has been severed between the 'expert' with the technical know-how and the common man.

CHAPTER 6

October 1972 Power To The People

In October 1972 I went to Mbeza to witness the final ceremony concluding the traditional mourning for the late Ila Chief Nalubamba, and the initiation of the new Chief Bright Nalubamba in his place.

This was a unique opportunity for me to witness one of the bravest attempts now being made in Zambia to graft the most modern concepts of rural development into the traditional structure of African life. The ba-Ila are no ordinary people, and the new Chief Nalubamba is no ordinary hereditary ruler. He presently holds the position of General Manager of Zambia's largest Credit Union, with a membership of 8,000 and total shares of over half a million kwacha (£250,000). He is entirely committed to the belief that the Co-operative Movement can become one of the most effective tools for the economic development of the rural areas of Zambia.

All the ba-Ila chiefs were there: Mukobela, Shezongo, Kaingu and Muwezwa from across the Kafue river. We sat under a grass awning outside the old chief's house, and the crowds began to gather making a circle in the centre of which the chief mourners shuttled back and forth, sometimes shouting, sometimes crooning their praise songs for the departed. Bare breasted women with white clay smeared on their faces reminded the spectators of the Chief's past glories and all his wealth of children. The men performed dances which described his cattle, using crooked arms and up-turned hands to show the length and shape of his oxen's horns. One diminutive and wizened old man with furious face and staring eyes brandished his hunting spears so viciously that those on the edge of the crowd drew back in fear lest he might forget they were flesh and blood, not the ghosts of the dead chief's enemies.

The day grew hotter, the crowd increased, the air filled with dust churned by dancing feet. The rich smell of cattle dung and cooking meat, mixing with the sweet stench of insaku tailings made us feel we were moving back in time to another world more real to us than the line of police land rovers and the plastic crates of bottled beer and sickly Coke. The beating of drums and the noise of happy people talking filled our ears. At midday the dancers from the Namwala Secondary School arrived. Their coming had been awaited with some excitement because they are recognised as the best dancers in the whole of Southern Province. We were not disappointed. They put on a display of traditional dancing such as I have never seen equalled during all my time in Zambia.

Their vigour, their rhythm, their muscular control, their sheer ability to enjoy themselves, shone in them and captivated the crowd who ceased to be spectators and became participants. Their play-acting, especially their imitation of their elders, crippled us with laughter, and their exposè of witch doctors as clever confidence tricksters must have shaken the faith of the most ardent devotees of the magical arts.

Suddenly as I watched this generation of young Zambians expressing themselves totally through a rediscovery of their old culture, I realised that the whole astonishing effort of building Secondary Schools in remote rural areas is being amply justified. Not because it is going to produce the professional men and women and the technicians of the future, but because, almost by accident, young people in an age group that is reaching physical maturity have had a chance to discover for themselves what being a Zambian is really all about.

But the new Chief had planned the ceremony with deeper intent than to provide an arena for his youth to show off their prowess and shame their elders. He knows that in the Ila country the chiefs still exert great influence, and village head-men are by no means nonentities. Wealth is power, and the ba-Ila aristocracy who own the great herds of cattle that graze on the Kafue flats hold the key to the development of that area. Chief Nalubamba has declared his intention to develop his people by yoking the power of the traditional leaders to the modern plough of technical advancement. In order to demonstrate this in a practical way he has started to build a 'People's Chamber' near his court. He commissioned the Zambian architect, Mr E.C. Maane, to design a new building which would combine the best in modern and traditional design. Already over £1,000 has been raised by subscription. The foundations of the new building have been dug, concrete blocks have been made, and we watched the old Chief Mungaila lay the foundation stone.

I did not visit Mbeza again until August 1973 when I found them still working on the People's Chamber.

CHAPTER 7

September 1973 Chiloto Bus

My second trip from Lusaka to Chipapa in 1966 was on a bicycle. I wanted to find out whether I could commute each day to work using this method of cheap transport. It took me two and a quarter hours to get there in the morning, and two and a half to get back in the evening because I got caught in a rain storm, and a lot of the way is uphill. Just one journey was enough to prove to me that cycling might be cheap, but it was too wasteful of time and energy. The next occasion I went was in my wife's little ten-year-old Ford Popular. That was much better. I think the most powerful argument made by the Chipapa people when they discussed whether I should be allowed to live in the village, was simply that any man with a car is an enormous asset to the community.

I was to be the only car owner in the whole area, and the consequences of that I was soon to discover, for the sun never rose but it revealed a little huddle of people with their bundles at my caravan door needing lifts to the clinic at Chilanga or to town.

The Ford Popular was made in Britain after the second world war as the people's utility car, and if anyone needed to be persuaded of the quality of British workmanship at that time, he should have seen us chugging up the hills to Lusaka with two on the bucket seat beside me in the front, and four behind, and the boot flap down piled high with bundles.

The first lesson I had to learn is that there is no such thing as a 'private' car in a village. It has to be a people's car, but mine was too small and more were left behind than I could take. Then I had a stroke of luck, I was given the temporary use of a two-ton Dyna Diesel. The village carpenter helped me make wooden seats in the back, and everyone rejoiced because no one was ever left behind on the road, and everyone who wanted it got a free ride into town in the morning, and a free ride back. That is everyone rejoiced but me. It is one thing to feel virtuous as the village saviour, but quite another to be at everyone's beck and call in any emergency from hospitalising pregnant women in the middle of the night, to taking mourners to a funeral on Saturday afternoon. There were problems too with the police who simply could not believe that I was not running a lucrative private bus service, and when I stopped at the South End roundabout in Lusaka to pick up my returning Chipapa passengers, all the other people waiting there wanting lifts to Chilanga and Kafue climbed aboard, and it might take half an hour to persuade them to get off. If they persisted I just had to carry them and keep stopping all along the road, and the Chipapa passengers would get furious with the delay because the women had promised to get back to cook their husbands' evening meal, and I didn't want to start breaking up the Chipapa marriages.

My problem was temporarily solved when I walked out of the situation and went back to Britain for a few months to front Christian Aid's World Poverty Campaign, but I took Chipapa's problem with me, because the people had been put right back where they were before; as they said 'crying for transport'.

By 1971 we had begun to work out together in our Ward Development Committee what we thought could be a possible solution to the problem which loomed larger and larger in the minds of the people as they began to need transport to get their produce to market. Here is a statement of our thinking at that time:

A. The Need
The people of Chipapa are in great need of transport for the following reasons:
1. To get children and their mothers and old people to the clinic at Chilanga.
2. To get seriously sick people to hospital in Lusaka in good time.
3. To enable relatives to go to Lusaka to visit sick people or when a person has died.
4. To get vegetables and chickens and eggs to the Lusaka market.
5. To do shopping.
6. To catch the train or bus in Lusaka when making a journey to a far place.
7. To get supplies of more things such as soap, paraffin, sugar, matches and candles for sale in the small local shops.

B. The Problem
1. The Chipapa road is not served by any kind of public transport. The United Bus Company of Zambia cannot agree to run a service until the number of regular passengers increases.
2. The distance is only twenty miles from Chipapa School to Lusaka, but not enough people travel each day to make it economic to make more than one journey to town each day.
3. Some days too many people want to travel and on other days there are very few.
4. Most people who are sick, especially women with sick children cannot afford to pay money every time they go to the clinic at Chilanga for treatment.
5. If a full-time driver is employed and given a proper monthly wage, he will spend all day in town doing nothing, but he

will expect to be paid for sitting and doing nothing.

6. If a small vehicle is used for transporting people and their bundles, it will often leave many people standing by the roadside without help. If a big vehicle is used, it is very expensive to buy and to keep running, and often it will run half empty. A taxi is too small and a bus too big.

C. A Possible Solution

The problem has been discussed with many people including the Road Traffic Commissioner to discover all about the legal side of running a bus service. The long term solution would be for one man to set up a transport business, and a garage and run an efficient bus service for the people, or the Bus Company should do it. However it will be some years before it becomes economic for one man to run a service, and the bus company cannot run a service on a route with few passengers when there are not even enough buses on the main routes and in the towns.

The people of Chipapa who are able to take vegetables and other things to market can afford to pay some money and also people earning salaries such as teachers, but the whole cost cannot be met by the people.

TRANSPORTATION TO AND FROM CHIPAPA MUST BE SOMEHOW SUBSIDISED OVER THE NEXT FIVE OR SIX YEARS.

When the prosperity of the area increases, the people will be able to afford to pay the full cost of a bus service. A bus service can be subsidised in a number of ways. The most important being:

a. No one person, or group of persons should make a profit out of this service to the people.

b. The richer and more educated members of the Chipapa community should offer help and assistance to those who are poor and sick.

c. Outside people can be asked to give help in buying the first vehicle. The Central Government, or Rural Council, or a charitable agency could be asked to help with the money.

It is now proposed that the Ward Development Committee should do the following:

a. Seek in every possible way to find £1,000 for the purchase of a strong pick-up truck (about 1.5 tons).

b. Find one trustworthy person in the community who would take charge of the vehicle making sure that it is properly serviced and kept in good order.

We had felt the need, we had analysed the problem, and we had made our plan, but the plan did not work. The reasons why it did not work were not first of all financial and technical, they were 'people' problems. We thought that the Ward Development Committee was the proper place to thrash out the issue and that the Ward was the right community to handle it, but we were wrong. Ward seventeen was created for Local Government electoral purposes. It was created by people who drew lines on maps to enclose a certain number of voters, but those boundaries took no notice of needs and aspirations of the people who lived within them. Ward seventeen is made up of two separate and distinct communities those of Chipapa and Chipongwe. The Chipapa people live in the seven little villages round the dam, and the centre of their life is the school and irrigated garden. They occupy the land under the customary law of usage, and they are all knit together in an inextricable web of family and kinship relationships. The Chipongwe people on the other hand are immigrants from many different tribes living on old state land farms owned by absentee landlords. Legally they are 'squatters'. As they live nearer to the main tar road running north to Lusaka and south to Kafue they have access to the state bus service, and they can get 'Zamcabs' and private taxis in an emergency.

When we divided the Ward up into nine sections, and appointed leaders in each section to explain the idea of raising money for a bus by every family subscribing £1.00 they all agreed, but when the time came to put the money on the table, the Chipongwe people all said that their existence as squatters was so precarious that they might be moved before the bus was bought, and so they would lose their money. The Chipapa people said that if the Chipongwe people did not subscribe they could not possibly reach the target; and then a big argument developed about whether a man with two or more wives should pay more than £1.00. Some said that a man with two wives was richer because he had more labour to work his gardens, and so could afford to pay more, others said that a man with two wives was poorer, because he had more children to support. They managed very effectively to avoid making a decision about their problems.

But all this time the problem was growing, the Chipapa people were getting desperate to find some way of getting their tomatoes, cabbages, peas, and beans to market, and although I would help whenever I could, I was often away for weeks at a time.

More and more people were travelling the road, and at this point two separate ideas began to emerge. First, the Chipapa people said that although they could not themselves raise the £1,000 needed, if they could get a loan to buy a second hand vehicle and get a driver, they would be able to pay off the loan from the money they would get transporting their vegetables to market. That was one idea. The other came from a man in the area who saw a chance of making some money out of the situation. Of course the two ideas ultimately came into conflict, but let me tell you what happened.

Our local 'rich man' found out that he could get a loan for two thirds of the capital required to buy a mini-bus from the government if he would put down the other third, and if he could get a franchise from the Road Service Commissioner for the route in question. He thought that there would not be enough passengers from the Chipapa and Chipongwe areas alone to make it pay so he applied for an extended route to serve the people right down at Chiaba on the Zambezi on two days a week, and serve the local people on the other five. He found he could purchase a sixteen seater mini-bus for £2,500 so he sold his herd of cattle to get his equity of £800 and bought the bus. He employed as a driver a cheerful young man who said he had a PSV licence, and was an experienced mechanic. He also took on another young man as conductor to collect the fares. Everyone was delighted and the bus was on the road from early morning until late at night. The more it travelled, the more passengers used it and the more money came in, even though sometimes it travelled half empty.

Meanwhile I was able to help the Chipapa vegetable growers get hold of a second hand one ton pick-up with a wooden canopy and a roof rack. If they packed it tightly they could carry in the vehicle eight passengers sitting on the floor, and up to half a ton of vegetables on the roof. Their main problem now was to find a driver. They had a meeting and said whoever drove their vehicle must be good with a clean licence, he must be absolutely honest, and he must be known never to touch beer. The trouble was that they thought they would never find such a person unless he would come down out of heaven. In fact there was one man in the village who had a driving licence, so they took him on even though they could only offer to pay him 50p a day.

He did marvellously for one week, and then he did not come home one night until very late, and it was found that he had been using the vehicle as his own private taxi when he got to town. So they said,

"We had better start at the other end. We will find a man who does not drink and is as honest as any man can be in this wicked world, and we will teach him to drive."

There was a man called Mr Phiri who had married a local woman. He used to work in a Lusaka bakery, but he had moved to Chipapa where he had built a little shop. It was not a very successful enterprise, because he always seemed to run out of stocks of candles and matches and sugar and salt just when people wanted them. We asked Mr Phiri if he would agree to be our driver if we could teach him to drive. He had never held the steering wheel of a car before, but he said he would try, and he started taking lessons in Lusaka. He did not pass the driving test the first time, but he did the second, and he began cautiously to drive the old pick-up to Lusaka every day.

I wanted him to take over from me the emergency trips that I sometimes had to make at night, but I never seemed to find the time to take him out at night to show him how to handle the van in the dark. One evening the sun set and Mr Phiri had not arrived home. Someone told me that he had taken the car up the valley the nine miles to the school at Chilambila to collect some teachers who had sent word that they needed him. I was surprised that he had the nerve to drive along that narrow twisting road through the hills, crossing the stony stream beds, and climbing up out of the drifts. Anyway, I thought, he will be sleeping there, and he will drive back in the morning, so I went to bed. I had no sooner put the light out, than I heard the familiar sound of the pick-up's engine, but I was puzzled because there was no light coming in through the window on that side of the house. I went outside and Mr Phiri was just locking the car door.

"That must have been quite a drive" I said "first time you

have ever driven at night."

"Yes" he said "I couldn't go very fast, that is why I am a bit late. The head and sidelights failed so I had to drive using the flashing indicators."

Mr Phiri looked after the car very well, always checking the oil and washing it down on Sunday morning, but one day the engine developed a knock. We towed it into the garage at Makeni and when they stripped it down, they told us that a most unusual thing had happened - one of the pistons had disintegrated, and the repair would cost over £250.

Our vehicle was off the road for two months but the local 'rich man' was laughing. He fixed a roof rack onto his mini-bus, and carried the vegetables to market, but he didn't laugh for long, because while his young driver was having the time of his life careering back and forth between Chiaba and our village and Lusaka he didn't worry too much about checking the oil, and he always believed that the faster you drive and the more journeys you could make, the more passengers you could carry and the more money you could jingle in your pocket. The mini-bus was not really designed for country roads, it was made for the cities and within a few months the engine was worn out. However many times the young driver took it to pieces laying the parts carefully on the dusty ground, and putting them back with new bearings or shims or con rods, it never worked again. So the rich man lost all his cattle, and all the money he had taken was spent on petrol and overtime to his driver and the bus conductor, and in the end of course he could not pay back his loan so the finance company had to repossess the bus and sell it for what they could get. No doubt in their annual report they will blame the 'irresponsible borrower' for not paying his debts, but they will write it off and lead some other poor sucker up the garden path never bothering to take care to find out whether he has the experience to manage a tricky thing like a transport business. But most of the blame should lie with the garage which sold him the mini-bus. All they cared about was to get the vehicle out of their glossy showroom, and get the money from the sale of the cattle, and the loan from the finance company safely into their own pockets, and the pockets of the mini-bus manufacturers in Europe and Japan.

But even when the Chipapa people got their vehicle back on the road again, (and they did not have any competition from the 'rich man'), they were not quite out of the wood. They were doing remarkably well and paying their way - that is all the running costs, and they were beginning to pay off their loan, but this meant packing the back of the vanette with the maximum number of people possible. People just had to get to town, even if it meant dropping down the tail board and sitting with their legs dangling a few inches from the ground. Quite rightly the police could not allow this to go on, and they finally impounded the car and took Mr Phiri to see Mr Banda the Road Traffic Commissioner. He just said flatly,

"Never more than three in the back and one passenger with the driver in front."

There were no two ways about it. We just had to get a bigger bus. It was then that I suffered my great temptation. When I came into town in the morning I would see the officials of the Bank of Zambia being driven to work in mini-buses, and the National Brewing Company had built a great big seven ton, forty seater to transport their staff to the brewery. All these people could have cycled to work if they had to. But the women of Chipapa, even if they wanted to, cannot cycle to market with their tomatoes, nor carry sick children to the clinic at Chilanga. I longed to give the poor of Chipapa their own spanking new bus with twice as much chromium plate as the Bank of Zambia bus.

I wanted to dress Mr Phiri in a chauffeurs' uniform with gold braided epaulettes and a blue peaked cap and white kid gloves. And I could have done if I had tried. All that was needed was a well worded, heart-string-tugging letter to Christian Aid or Oxfam - that was my temptation, but I kicked the devil in the crutch and did the right thing. I started working with the members of the little Credit Union in the village and said that if only they would start saving the money they were making from their vegetables, and if they would really work at it, and pull together and save, they could get the money for the down payment on a new bus. They are not that poor. Some of them have got cattle and if they really put their minds to it they could do it. But they didn't. For the peasants of Chipapa there is no tomorrow for which you can save to day. They have learned by bitter experience that the future is dark with impending calamity. If you can manage to store away a little money in a hole in the ground, it must be kept hidden in a secret place, only to be brought out in time of dire need which means great sickness or the death of someone in the family. They knew that the little pick-up was too small, they knew that sooner or later it would break down or wear out, they knew it was running illegally, but as long as Mr Phiri kept it going they would put off the need to raise money for a new one. I knew we had to have a new vehicle, and I knew it was not any good handing it to the people on a plate, because they had to feel it was their own and that they had worked to get it, so I began to talk with them about what they knew they needed.

They knew that a mini-bus (like the rich man's mini-bus) was not the answer. It must be bigger but not too big. It must be strong enough to stand the bashing it would get on the Chipapa road, but not as big as the brewery bus. We began to get a picture of what we needed. It should be a three tonne chassis with a Zambian made body, built to our requirements. It must have a door at the back with a bench with seats for ten down each side with a seat for two or three across the end with their backs to the cab. There must be windows down both sides, but not windows that open, because those are much too expensive. The two windows up front would simply be left as open spaces to let the air in. The main floor space must be left free so that people could pile in their boxes of tomatoes and bags of cabbages and beans, and crates of chickens and even a bicycle or two if necessary. With plenty of floor space the bus could be used on Saturdays to take the football teams for matches at the neighbouring schools. I began making enquires in Lusaka from the garages to see what a three ton chassis would cost. They said £2,500. I went to the engineering firms to see what it would cost to build on a custom made body. they said £1,000 but with the price of steel going up it might be £1,500 in a few months' time. The situation was utterly hopeless because even if the people managed to raise £500 and we got a finance company to give us a loan for the rest, they would demand repayment over two years at 12.5%, and we should never be able to pay it off. We would have to find something cheaper. A motor company had recently opened up a new branch in Lusaka Road. I went to enquire about the price of a chassis and explained what we needed. The manager gave me a funny look and said,

"I've got something in the back that might interest you, come and see."

I walked into the new big shed at the back. It was like one of those huge empty warehouses you see on a dock side waiting for a shipment of goods. Standing right in the middle of this great commercial cathedral was our dream bus, made exactly to our plan. There it stood, all new, and blue, and shining in the morning sun which filtered through the transparent corrugated fanlights in the roof. I asked,

"Who did you make it for?"

He said "Its a bit of a sad story. We made it for one of the mining companies up on the Copperbelt to carry their workers, and sent it up there, but they sent it back. They said it was no use because the windows don't open and there is not enough ventilation for the people travelling inside. Besides, the mine workers union wouldn't pass a home made thing like that! I'm afraid there is nothing for it, but to take the body off and replace it with a flat bed body and sell it as an ordinary truck."

"How much do you want for it?" I asked,

"£2,750." he said.

I had got to find two thousand seven hundred and fifty pounds and find it quickly if the Chipapa dream was going to come true. But that sort of money doesn't grow on trees. If only I had a rich friend to give us a temporary loan until we could organise the money. But the rich don't travel our road in Chipapa, so we never meet them there to make them our friends. Then I remembered that round the corner from the garage where the blue bus stood in all its glory, was a very rich man.

We were friends when we had once been poor together, in the early days at Mumbwa. I was then an impecunious missionary, he was a business man with too many irons in the fire, and none red hot. Well some of his irons in the end did get hot, red hot, so his problem became not how to make money, but how to put his money to good use. I was already in debt to this man, not because he had ever made me a loan, but because he saved me from becoming a one hundred percent socialist. When I see the 'wicked' white capitalists exploiting the poor downtrodden peasants, then I am sometimes tempted to declare that Zambia's only path to economic sanity must be the nationalization road. But when I stop talking about the 'masses' and start talking to Daniel and Sarah and the others, I find that they get a much better deal from that 'wicked' white capitalist who is my friend, than from the giant para-statal transport organisation which competes with him in the same way of business. The other thing is that while he has grown rich by running an efficient and well jacked-up family business, it has cost the government millions of pounds to run their undisciplined, extravagant, and over-staffed para-statal. So although capitalism has its ugly face in Zambia, it is really no uglier than the state's monsters whose towering concrete castles disfigure the human face of Cairo Road in Lusaka.

So I went round the corner to see him, and there he was - not in a carpeted and air conditioned room on the fifteenth floor of the latest Lusaka sky scraper, but in his dusty office at 'the yard' surrounded by his yellow painted trucks and trailers and tankers. I had to pass through no protective screen of busily chatting typists, I walked straight through the open door of his office and said,

"Jukes, I have found me a truck and I want you to buy it for me."

"What do you mean you want me to buy you a truck?" "Well its not really for me, its for the Chipapa people, and I don't really want you to buy it, I just want you to lend us the money."

"Bit of a risk isn't it to put a truck in the hands of a bunch of villagers who can hardly look after their own bicycles, and have never driven anything faster than an ox cart. Anyway, how much do you want, and how are you going to pay me back? I've always said I'm prepared to help anyone who can show me he is helping himself, Anyway where is it? I'm not going to let you buy a pig in a poke. Let's go and see it."

So we went round to see it in the big empty warehouse.

It was standing over an open inspection pit, so he got down underneath and had a good look at the suspension.

"How much is he asking for it?"

"Only £2,750 and a new one would cost £4,000 and..." "Too much" he said "I'll knock him down by £250"

"But supposing someone else comes in and offers him a bit more?"

"Don't be daft man. He wouldn't be asking £2,750 if it's worth not a penny more than £2,500. What I have got to decide is whether I can take the risk of knocking him down by four hundred not two fifty."

I kept my fingers crossed while he was making up his mind!

Jukes made the deal which I thought was a very fair one (and one that other rich men might do worse than to follow), he said that for every pound invested by the people of Chipapa in their bus he would invest another pound. Remember, the people at that point had raised nothing.

Now I faced the big question. What would the people of Chipapa do? I took the leaders and some of the elders to see the shining bus. At first they couldn't believe their eyes and said it must be a gift from heaven.

"No way" I said.

"It belongs to the man in the garage and he will only sell it to us if we in Chipapa make a really serious effort to get the money to put down a substantial deposit."

They said they would go back to Chipapa and discuss it with the people and let me know. I gave them two weeks, and said we would meet on Sunday 30th June at nine o'clock and there must be no promissory notes. All that the man at the garage was interested in was hard cash.

When the time came for the meeting, I went to the courthouse, but nobody came. It had been a cold night with hoarfrost in white patches on the ground, so people were in no hurry to crawl out of their blankets nor leave the sweet potatoes roasting in the warm embers of the previous night's fire. By ten o'clock they came straggling in, some with ten pound notes, some with five and some with only one pound in their hands. At ten o'clock Yoram Mwando, the retired cook who owns the grinding mill came forward out of the little crowd and laid a bundle of ten pound notes on the table. We counted them and there were ten of them - one hundred pounds! Everyone clapped and there was a buzz of conversation, then Elisa brought forty which she had saved from the sale of vegetables last year. Daniel went to get his Bible and started preaching about the talents. He was reading the words of the Master "Well done thou good and faithful servant" when Mr Phiri walked in. We all knew that none of us would ever have given a penny for the purchase of the bus unless we had confidence in our servant the driver, and he showed the confidence he had in himself, and in them, by laying his hundred pounds on the open pages of the Bible.

By five o'clock that afternoon there were nine hundred and ninety nine pounds in the box. A doctor who came to visit us that day from Kitwe gave the last pound to make it a thousand, and we had sure promises of another three hundred which in fact was brought before the end of the week.

Everyone was very happy, because now we could go in the morning to collect the bus which had been waiting in the garage, but still a little doubt was niggling at the back of my mind. We had done the sums over and over again, and in four years we could pay off the loan with interest if everything went smoothly. But I had heard that week, that the cost of petrol had been doubled, and with a three ton truck with a petrol engine, the cost of fuel is the major running cost. It looked as if the whole venture might come unstuck for a reason beyond our own control. If the vehicle cost so much to run that there would be no "profit" each week to pay back the loan, then the promises we had made to the investors, that is the people, and Jukes, would all be empty, and the people would blame the driver, and Jukes would say

"I told you so".

In fact although the Chiloto bus ran very successfully for some years, Mr Phiri found the responsibility of being both driver/mechanic and collector of fares all too much for him. He resigned and the new driver was not such an honest man. Rampant inflation drove up the cost of repairs and maintenance and finally the dream faded away, and the bus ended up in a Lusaka scrap heap. Jukes Curtis never did get his money back.

CHAPTER 8

A visit from a wild goose and a parliament of birds

We were expecting guests over the weekend, so Sarah killed the last of our little flock of Emden geese. It was a big bird, too large to go into my little oven, so Sarah stewed it on her open fire for six hours, which was just as well, because the flesh was tough as old boots. But it made the most delicious soup I have ever tasted, and was more than enough for all the visitors who came.

On Sunday early in the morning Sarah knocked on my door and said,

"A stranger has arrived."

"Where is he?" I asked

"In the chicken run"

"What do you mean - a stranger in the chicken run?"

"It's not a man, it's a bird" she said.

"Did it fly in?"

"No, she just came walking down the path and stood outside the gate asking to be let inside to feed with the hens and the Muscovy ducks."

I walked over to the hen run and there she was, a beautiful spur-winged goose. How the sun glistened on her black and purple wings. How proudly she held her head above that splendid neck of hers. She was a wild goose, who looked at us with steady eye seeming strangely to show no trace of fear.

Sarah's husband Daniel, rubbing sleep from his eyes came out of the house to see the stranger. I caught him looking round for a stick to clobber her. Daniel the hunter saw no thing of beauty there, just meat for a hungry man. And who was I to blame him? Once I had killed a wild hare which had become trapped on the veranda of my house, jumping through an open window in the moonlight. I had killed it with my bare hands for then I too was poor and in need of meat. As we watched the wild goose eyeing us, curving down her slender neck to feed, I knew that we were not to kill her. In fact she stayed with us for a full month, flying down to the dam each morning to bathe, and preen her feathers and graze along the margin of the lake, returning each evening to eat the grain scattered on the ground for the Muscovies and to sleep with them at night. One day three wild geese came in at dawn. They landed on the water of the lake and there she joined them. In the evening they all flew away westwards to the Kafue river into the flame of the sun at its setting.

On the morning of the first day of July, I went for a walk by the dam. The temperature had dropped below zero in the night. Patches of white hoarfrost were melting in the warmth of a sun whose slanting rays gave every tree a halo and spun a glittering canopy across the silvery tops of the papyrus reeds around the lake. Suddenly I was aware of a great celebration such as I have never seen or heard before. It was going on all around me. Overhead a pair of eagles were gliding high on silent wings, then from the west, from behind Chipapa's hill, came beating in a single cormorant only a little lower in the heavens than the eagles. When he reached the point directly above the dam where his mate dried her wings, perched on the branch of a fallen tree amongst the reeds, he spiralled down to within a foot of the water's surface, then levelling out he skimmed the whole circumference of the lake. I heard a lourie calling from the top of one of the mimosa trees but all I could see was his head with the grey crest rising and falling silhouetted against the sun. There seemed to be a bird on the topmost branch of every tree. A dove alighted on a high twig right next to a grey sparrow hawk. A pair of barbetts flew from tree to tree, beating out their boundaries with their see-saw call of warning.

The blue jays had stopped their monotonous scolding of the black and white crows. Climbing vertically into the sky above their tree they came swooping down, sunlight shining through their azure wings. The birds of Chipapa don't sing as sweetly as the birds of England sing; they have no need, for their music is in their colour and their flight. Even so, on that morning in July, the air was full of bird song. The liquid notes of the bulbuls were everywhere and the soft call of the pigeons came from the fig trees, the high cry of the eagles and the sound of the plovers answering one another across the water enraptured me; made me stand to listen as to some ancient hymn.

What I saw that morning I have never seen before nor have I seen again. It was one of those great gatherings of birds around the lake, the accounts of which are still preserved in the folklore of Zambia. It was not the number of the birds, though there were as many as I have ever seen before, it was their variety. It was like a parliament with every species sending its own representatives. A sandpiper flew up from under my feet. From the reeds came the first lillytrotters with white breasts and chestnut wings, trailing their long legs behind them as they flew, and a moorhen skimming so low it marked a V-trail across the ripples of the lake. The pied kingfisher hovered motionless on wings which beat so fast you scarcely saw their movement, then suddenly, like a falling stone, one would plummet and rise again, a silver fish in its jet black beak. Amongst the reeds I saw the flash of a malachite kingfisher as she came to rest on her fishing perch, a reed bent horizontal just above the water. For a long time I watched this tiny creature and marvelled that God had bothered to make so small a thing so very beautiful.

On the muddy shore were the plovers which look so undistinguished, so dapper while they walk by the water's edge

93

for all the world like the civil servants who walk the corridors of the Ministry of Legal Affairs, but when they take off in flight are transformed into a kaleidoscope of beating wings, all orange and black and white and grey. Our great white egret who fishes from a mudbank was joined by the big grey heron from the other side. They seemed to be carrying on a very long and serious discussion about nothing. I have never seen them stand so close before and as I watched there came on lazy wings a great and glorious bird, a giant heron whose plumes glowed like molten copper from the sun's smelter. He came that day and walked majestically along the shore looking for frogs and other things to eat, but I have not seen him again and I'm afraid that the schoolboys with their catapults may have frightened him away for ever.

Our lake is not a natural stretch of water, it was man-made twenty years ago, and the men who made the dam were certainly interfering with nature. Twenty years ago there were no cormorants, herons, kingfishers or lillytrotters, wattled plovers moorhens or coots. Yet now they are here, and they have come as the wild goose came to bless this place.

On that morning by our little lake I did not understand what the meaning was of that great celebration. I did not know what the birds were trying to tell me. It was not until I got to town that I knew. There I saw the buses jammed full of people going to work, and I saw the great crowds of children assembling outside their steel and concrete schools. They are growing up without knowing the name of a single bird, except perhaps the drongos on the roof tops, and the sparrows which eat the bread crumbs round the tricycles of the Coca Cola sellers.

We have separated our children from the creation, we have made it almost impossible for them to be meek, so how shall they inherit the earth? We make them into hooligans who turn to violence to snatch their own reward. How I should love to be able to take one of those children from the town school and put a pair of binoculars in her hand, and show her a malachite kingfisher with red beak poised quite still on his bent reed above the water. Why should that privilege be preserved for the children of the rich American tourists who come to visit our game parks, to click their cameras hoping to carry our peace back with them to their restless homes? And then I thought,

"Why just one child? Why shouldn't they all come to Chipapa?"

Instead of Mr Phiri sitting all morning in town waiting for his passengers to get their shopping done, and grow fat sipping endless bottles of Coca Cola, why shouldn't he fill the bus with kids, and take them for a morning's excursion to the village? After all, isn't this what it is really all about? How we can find a way of bridging the widening gap between town and country, rich and poor, the meek and the violent. Up to that Wednesday morning, I had always thought of our dream bus as being a link between Chipapa and the town, but now I understood what the birds were saying, "Use your bus to bring the children of the town to see us here, let them feel the gold dust of their inheritance run through their fingers. Let them drink the milk and taste the honey."

CHAPTER 9

August 1973 Visit to Mbeza

A few months before I left Zambia for good I went back to Mbeza for my farewell party. There were twenty five of us in the Chipapa Chiloto bus of whom six were traditional Headmen. We met this time under the fig tree outside the new council chamber. It still was not quite finished, but the architect was there with a hammer in his belt and a mouthful of nails putting up the ceiling in the spacious room where the Chief would meet his people, the headmen of his forty villages and other leaders in the community, the Chairman and Board of the 'Mbeza people's Bank', the manager of the Mbeza Consumers' Co-operative Society (with subscription capital of £5,000), the Director of the 'Women's Development Brigade', the Health Committee members, and the Government Veterinary and Agricultural Officers.

On this occasion the Chief had no need to invite the dance troupe from the Secondary School. He has divided his area into ten sections, and each section sends its best dancers to the Mbeza Cultural and Dancing Troupe. There must have been three or four hundred of us there on that hot Sunday afternoon all gathered in the shade of the great fig tree. No beer had been brewed, and no oxen killed, but everyone had put on their gayest clothes and we had a party which was as good as any party on the State House lawn in Lusaka. There were only two drummers, but how they made their drums talk! There was one story teller who told us the funniest shaggy dog story I have ever heard - all to the accompaniment of the drum and mimicry of yapping dogs and baying dogs and snarling dogs and growling dogs. The dancers were neither very old nor very young, except for one six month old baby on her mother's back whose head jiggled up and down throughout the dance and who clapped in gleeful delight whenever her mother held her hands above her head. There was a large puppet doll manipulated by a prone woman swathed in coloured cloth. She was supposed to be anonymous but she giggled so much all the crowd had discovered her identity almost before the show began.

The high moment came when the chief dancer came forward all dressed in coloured beads and skins of cerval cats. He had a black briefcase in one hand, and a dancer's reed - and - bottletop skirt in the other. He laid them on the table in front of us, and out of his briefcase he took a complete telephone, black stand and receiver, with a wire which he took down under the table. There was no buzzer so one of the dancing girls came forward with a cow bell. The bead bedecked dancer dialled a number and the bell rang,

"Give me international exchange please"

he said, and the man who was sitting on the ground under the table at the other end of the line replied,

"What number do you want?"

"The manager of the National Bank of Switzerland."

"And where are you calling from, and what is your number?"

"Mbeza 253 - you ought to know my number by now."

All this time the drums were beating softly and the rhythm of the dance went on. There was much tapping of the button on the receiver stand and much tinkling of the bell and crackle from the man under the table.

"Hello, hello, hello. Is that the Bank of Switzerland? I want to speak to the manager please. Hello, hello, hello."

"Just hold on a minute, I'm trying to put you through... the manager is on the line."

"Good morning sir... very well thank you and hoping you...

everything is very fine up here in Mbeza. I just thought I would give you a ring and tell you that developments are going on very well here. Mbeza is at a high consciousness of development... thank you very much sir, I must ring off now, so many people are queueing up to deposit their money..."

The bell tinkled and the drummers stepped up the tempo of their beat. People in the crowd ran into the centre of the circle to join the song and dance, the clapping and the stamping of their feet became a symphony of rhythm, a music of delight. The chief dancer still sitting at the table had put down the phone, and was giving his entire attention to his typewriter. The dancing skirt made up of threaded reeds and bottle tops, under his expert fingers gave out a sound for all the world like any ancient Underwood or Adler. All to the rhythm of the drums, he rang the bell, and moved the carriage back, and whipped invisible sheets of paper from imaginary rollers.

This whole performance was put on for my benefit because for some years I had been National Chairman of the Board of Directors of C.U.S.A. (The Credit Union Savings Association of Zambia). This movement grew rapidly after Independence and Chief Nalubamba, one of our most enthusiastic board members wanted me to see how successfully it had taken root in the villages of his chieftaincy. I stood up and congratulated the chief and his people on the amazing progress of 'Mbeza People's Bank' and then I got a great surprise.

I had let it be known amongst my friends that when I returned to England I would ask the Methodist Church for their continuing support for the new nation of Zambia. In particular for the Ba-Ila because the church's first missionaries who crossed the Zambezi in 1889 called themselves "Ba-Ila Ba-Tonga Mission of the Primitive Methodist Church". However, I said half jokingly, the educational standard of the English is so high that no one takes any notice of what you say unless you can call yourself a professor or a doctor. I coveted the title 'doctor' but Dr Kaunda who was Chancellor of the University of Zambia never took the hint, even though he himself had an honorary doctorate. I need not have worried because Chief Nalubamba had heard the whisper.

As the clatter of the typewriter fell silent three men stepped forward from the band of dancers. The first carried an imitation ceremonial lion spear (if it had been for real it would have been smeared with lions blood). The second carried a calabash decorated with coloured beads for casting bones. The third held a white sacrificial cock with tied legs and flapping wings. The Chief moved forward and said, "Merfyn Temple, with these insignia of office I confer upon you the honorary doctorate of my Ba-Ila tribes. After your name you may add the letters D.Ex (Doctor of Experience)".

Return to the First World

I left Africa in 1974 and came to live in England where I suffered severe culture shock for two years before settling down to become the minister of All Saints Methodist Church in Abingdon near Oxford. In 1982 I retired and became a grower of organic fruit and vegetables on an acre and a half of borrowed land in the village of Upper Basildon not far from Reading in Berkshire.

My life in Africa had become a half forgotten dream until one day out of my past came a grey haired Zambian friend named Job Mayanda at that time working at the Zambia High Commission in London but still in close contact with conditions in Zambia. He invited me to visit Africa again to help in finding an alternative to farming with hybrid maize seed and chemical fertilizers. So in 1989 I set out to travel with a bicycle from Nairobi to Kariba to see if my newly discovered enthusiasm for ecological agriculture might be of any help. The story of that journey was published under the title 'New Hope For Africa'. Chapter 7 of that book (diary for Nov 1989) recounts my visit to Chipapa en route to the Zambezi valley so I have reproduced it here.

CHAPTER 10

November 24th 1989 Return to Chipapa

Today I came to Chipapa. Nothing seems to have changed, though the bougainvillea bush on the right of the veranda has grown into a tree whose branches provide cool shade over half the house. The one on the left has climbed thirty feet to the top of a musekese tree, making a cascade of purple blossom to hide the rusting body of the yellow Toyota pick-up, which we used to take vegetables from the irrigated garden to the market in Lusaka. A skinny black cat with three even skinnier kittens tugging at her, licked her shabby black fur. No one had ever fixed the window-frame I gave Daniel into the cavity he left for it when he built his house twenty years ago. The iron railway-sleeper still propped up the piece of battered tin he had found to fill the hole. The blackened straw on Sarah's kitchen still covered half the roof, the rest had been pulled out to light the kitchen fire.

I walked down to the dam, and the sight of its blue waters took my breath away. Chipapa is still for me one of the most beautiful small places in the world. Everything looked the same. A few women were fishing, the older children sat chatting and laughing in the shade of the makoka trees, the younger ones had made long thick ropes of twisted grass which they used to sweep the shallow water on the lake's margin up the sloping sand, leaving tiny fish flipping their silver tails on the shore. A big herd of cattle came down to drink. Numbering at least two hundred, cows, calves, oxen and bulls, they all seemed to be in prime condition. I walked along the dam wall under the makoka and fig trees which have grown into a little forest right down to the edge of the water. Below the dam the guavas, the bananas, and the mango trees are all heavily laden with fruit.

The irrigated garden, where sixty families once cultivated their own small plots of land, had long ago been abandoned to the thorn trees and tall elephant grass. The big four-inch outflow pipe had become silted up and no one knew how to clear it. By the time I returned to the house Sarah and Daniel had arrived back from a funeral. Sarah's sweet smile was the same she gave me when I first arrived twenty years ago. I hardly knew Daniel, now almost blind, very deaf and moving uncertainly. We sat and talked about all the people who had died.

I asked what had happened to the vehicle we used to call the Dream Bus, because we had been able to purchase it in part with money given to us in a dream. They said it was lying 'buggered up' and tyreless in the no-man's land between the people of Kalambalala and the people of Mulendema. I was not surprised, because even when we ran the transport to get our vegetables to market, this bus had been a bone of contention between these two groups of feuding families. All Daniel wanted to do was to rake over and over again the ashes of that tawdry controversy. In order to change the subject, I asked how his nearest neighbour, Moses Zumbwa was getting on.

"He died six months ago" said Daniel "his son John, who worked as an agricultural assistant at Mt. Makulu, the Government Research Station ten miles away, has left his job and come to inherit his land with his two younger brothers."

I suggested we walk over so that I could give my condolences to the widow. We found John the son, desperately trying before the rains came to get a few corrugated-iron sheets put temporarily over part of a new house he is building from sun dried brick.

He offered me a seat on his buckskin-covered deck chair, drew up his stool and we began to talk. It was a relief for me to talk in English instead of my rusty Tonga, and to talk about the present rather than the past. Five young men emerged from the trees to join us. When I was here before I envied old man Moses Zumbwa for the site he had chosen to build his house. It is on a hillside above the lake, and looks out to the south over the top of a huge fig tree where we held the big Indaba with Kaunda in 1972, to celebrate the coming of the 'Green Revolution' to Chipapa. From this high point you look out across the Mpande hills, which stretch away for twenty miles to the Kafue river, where it runs through the Kafue gorge with the great Kafue hydroelectric power station on its banks.

I began to tell John Zumbwa and the five young men what this area was like when I first found it, exploring on my bicycle from Lusaka twenty years ago. I told them that it looked hardly any different from how it looks now, though the trees are taller, and the fields even more arid and desolate than they were then, though the herds of cattle look bigger and fatter. I told them how I brought the 'Green Revolution' and what a disaster it had been.

It was after the 'Green Revolution' had failed that we managed to get the outflow pipe in the dam wall mended and Chipapa's years of prosperity began. The people paid off their debts from the sale of tomatoes, peas, beans and irrigated maize. The rainy seasons got better, and they were able to purchase fertilizer again. The yields of grain went up but the soil began to get poorer. The drought returned, and the pipe in the dam wall got blocked again. A whole family died from drinking beer made in drums that had contained Agro chemicals. The drums were clearly marked 'POISON' but the people could not read. We are back where we started twenty years ago, though the soil is poorer now, and no amount of fertilizer will ever take us back again to a yield of twenty bags to the acre.

John Zumbwa and his young friends had nodded and grunted with agreement all through my story. They knew in their guts that every word was true. Then they told me something I did not know. They said,

"You remember, Muluti, that when you were here we used to take our cattle to graze in the woodlands of the Mpande Hills. You remember you once asked Godfrey Kalambalala the young herd-boy, how he could be up in the hills all day without water, and he told you there was a stream of 'white water' there. You went looking for it and you found a stream. Still standing by the side of it was an old smelting furnace made of clay where our great grandfathers made the iron for their spears, hoes and axes."

Now I was nodding and grunting my agreement.

"You remember how we made plans for a cattle-camp in those Mpande hills and an expert came to advise us about an insemination scheme to improve the quality of our beasts, but nothing came of these plans. Instead charcoal-burners arrived, first in twos and threes, and then they brought their families. From north, south, east and west they came, the Bemba and the Namwanga, the Luvale, the Lozi, and the Lunda, the Tumbuka and all the tribes up to Malawi. They came even from Tanzania. Every day we see the trucks passing here carrying big loads of charcoal up to Lusaka. Now there are more people living in the Mpande hills than in all the villages from Chipapa up to the railway line. Without the clothing of the trees the hillsides will be left naked."

I knew what they told me was true, because as we crossed the railway line at Chipongwe a Land Rover piled high with charcoal had passed by. On the hillsides there are no longer any trees, only the secondary growth of green from the hacked-away stumps. There was a long silence, then John Zumbwa spoke,

"As long ago as last May we heard you speaking from the radio on the BBC in London. We knew you would come, and we have already started making plans. We have cleared all the ground round the broken outflow pipe of the dam. A local European farmer has promised to help us, and now we are just waiting for him to come. We keep reminding him, and we will go to him again. I am the new chairman of the irrigated garden group. As soon as the water begins to flow, within a week everyone is ready to begin work on their plots. I have ploughing oxen and donkeys on the way. I have already dug a well here, and all we need is a pump to make our orchard and nursery for small trees. You ought to know that when you were here you could never persuade any young man to stay in the village to work the land, they all rushed off to find work in the towns. The only ones remaining were those with no education. They had no education because they were too lazy to learn in school. They were born lazy, and they live now as loafers sponging off their families. All that has changed. These five young men are only a few but they are all well-educated. There are many more like them in the villages. They have understood that living a life of unemployment in the towns is hard and difficult. Their uncles no longer want to feed them because the price of food keeps going up. They have now returned, and are waiting to be guided into ways of making a good living from the land".

Sarah came to call me for a bath, and it was the same tin bath she poured water into twenty years ago on the day of my arrival.

I was tired so went early to bed, the only light I had was a piece of string stuck through the lid of an ink bottle containing paraffin. At midnight I was woken by the clatter of tins and cups and saucers. Some animal seemed to be prowling clumsily along the kitchen shelves, next door to my bedroom. I lit the lamp and went into the kitchen. Sarah had left there a bowl of sugar and some hunks of bread in a basin covered by three saucers. As I entered the room I saw in the shadows dozens of rats and mice of all sizes climbing over the shelves, up the wires which suspended them from the rafters. For all the world they looked like the crew called out to man the yardarms of a clipper ship. I covered the sugar and the bread more securely, but as soon as the light went out the racket began all over again. I could not sleep, so took the lamp to the kitchen table and found that if I moved it across the page of my diary there was just enough of a glimmer to write a few words at a time. By 2 o'clock the rats and mice had stopped peering at me from behind the saucepans and plates and gone off to scavenge somewhere else.

I was up at 5:00a.m. determined to get on the road to Kafue before it got too hot. Sarah insisted on bringing me soft mealie-meal porridge, no milk of course, because all Daniel's cows are dead and gone. I had to shout our morning prayers, but even so the sick old man, who had once been in the forefront of the 'Green Revolution', knew no more than that we had knelt together. Perhaps that was enough. I set off on the bike for Kafue. As I cycled along the road people who had heard the rumour of my arrival ran out from their houses to greet me. One of them was the man who long ago brought his lantern through the darkness to help us to see where to cut the umbilical cord of a child who was born in the back of a pick-up, on the way to hospital. They called her 'Mukwakwa' 'The one who is born on the road'. Unhappily she was not there to greet me, as she died when she was only five years old.

'New Hope For Africa' continues the account of my journey into the Zambezi Valley where I came to lose my bicycle in the

trackless bush country between Syampondo and Livingstone, so I had to return to Britain without it. After two years without news I decided to go back and follow up some of the projects initiated on that previous visit, and to enquire for news of my abandoned cycle. In 1992 I returned. En route to the valley I once again visited Chipapa. My diary for February 8th and 9th 1992 records that visit as follows:-

A Brigadier General picks me up and takes me to Chipapa

The minor road to Chipapa which leaves the main road at this point serves only the villages and a few farms. There is very little traffic so as there would not be much chance of a lift, I set off to walk the seven miles to the village. As there was no one about and the midday sun was blazing hot, I put on my ridiculous hat. I had gone no more that a couple of hundred yards and was standing at the roadside when I saw a big saloon car coming slowly up behind me. There was one man in the driving seat and no passengers. I flagged him to stop, which he did.

The car was a highly polished silver grey Mercedes Benz with red plush seats and the driver was a pleasant looking man of about forty with a plump black face. He wore a khaki shirt of fine Egyptian cotton with something embroidered in gold thread on the pocket. He said that he would be glad to give me a lift but he had only a mile to go to his house and he had not heard of Chipapa. He told me that he had retired last December from the post of Brigadier General of the Zambia National Youth Service after twenty years of honourable service. I did not tell him that I had been one of the founders of the service in 1963, but in those days I was not called a Brigadier, I was simply called the Deputy Director. I had not retired taking with me my personal Mercedes Benz, I had been sacked with no pension because I had dared to suggest that the only future for the young men in

107

the service was to get them back to the land.

We came to his house which was surrounded by a ten foot concrete wall with a capping of vicious looking jagged glass. We drove through the massive iron gates, past the kennels of his fierce guard dogs, one of which I could see had been crossed with a pit bull terrier, up the concrete drive lined with orange trees to the front of the house where two other sleek saloon cars were parked. One was another Merc, and the other a Renault 2000. He offered me a comfortable chair on the spacious veranda and went inside to get me a bottle of iced Coca Cola. I peeped through the glass doors into the lounge and dining room. Two free standing electric fans played back and forth ruffling the edges of the embroidered antimacassars along two rows of lavishly upholstered settees and armchairs. The only picture on the walls was a full length colour photograph of the Brigadier himself in full dress army uniform, epaulettes dripping with gold braid.

He kindly offered to run me out to the village if I would show him the way. We had to change into the other Mercedes which had a higher clearance to lift it over the obstacles along the village road. Before we left he offered to show me round his orange groves which were irrigated with water from a large tank filled by a powerful electric pump from a deep bore hole .

The Brigadier had never been along the road before and exclaimed with surprise as we passed the cluster of whitewashed school buildings. We left the car at the roadside and walked the last hundred yards through the tall grass to my old house which is still there.

Through the trees we saw Sarah sitting by the kitchen fire with two young women. We announced our arrival with the call, "Odi! Odi!." They came over to welcome us and when Sarah saw that it was me, her face lit up and I gathered her into my arms.

I think the Brigadier was not only surprised but also embarrassed when he saw the house I had lived in. Compared with his it is indeed a shanty but this man has cut himself off from his own people by adopting a lifestyle which can only make them jealous of his unbelievable affluence. He did not stay long because we had little in common to talk about. As he got into his car the rain came down and we ran for shelter to my old house where we found a place to sit where no rain came through the roof.

A terrible drought but the dam is full

Daniel, was asleep in the house when we arrived. He is now almost totally blind and so deaf that only shouting into his ear can get a message through to his kindly mind, but his lips and wrinkled smile showed how pleased he was that I had come back. The two other women who came to welcome me were young and beautiful, Sarah's granddaughter and her niece. One of them went off to the house behind the mango trees to call John Zumbwa, the man in the village whom above all others I wanted to see.

On my last visit, in all my despair for Chipapa, it was John and the five young men with him who gave me hope. He is twenty years younger than I, clean limbed, spare and alert. We sat on the open veranda of my old house under the purple bougainvillea which I had planted twenty years ago. Through the trees we could see the sparkling water of the dam.

On my last visit I heard how the irrigation outlet pipe at the bottom of the dam wall had become blocked ten years before. The sixty families depending for their income on the water for their vegetable plots had slipped back into poverty again. John had told me that in 1989 he was working at the Mount Makulu

Agricultural Research Station. His father died and he had to take early retirement in order to come home to look after his mother who had become very ill. He wanted to help his people get the water flowing again, so he persuaded someone from the Department of Water Affairs to come and see the situation. They said they could do nothing, so he went to a white farmer in the area to ask for advice. This man said if the people would clear the bush around the blocked valve he would come to see what he could do but, in spite of repeated requests for help he never came.

John stood for election as councillor for the Chipapa ward of the District Council. During the election campaign he visited everyone including the local farmers who live between the railway line and the main road. One was a successful black South African woman farmer who is married to a Dane called Jansson who owns an engineering works in Lusaka. John outlined his proposals for the development of his Ward which included repair of the irrigation scheme. Jansson offered to go to Chipapa to see if there was anything he could do to help. As soon as he saw the situation, he realised that the dam had silted up over the years and that to unblock the pipe would be a major operation.

He said to John,

"I know what needs to be done and I believe if everyone in the village is prepared to work, we can get the irrigation system going again. I'll give you one week to mobilize the people with their axes and hoes, to clear all the bush round the dam wall and along the furrow into the garden. When I come back, if I see you are serious about getting the dam repaired, I'll tell you what we have to do next."

When he returned he could hardly believe his eyes. All the land had been laid bare, as though a bulldozer had scraped it clean.

110

He went to his drawing board and designed a new system of pipes which would allow for the blocked pipe to be cleared. He estimated all the costs including the hire of a compressor to pump out the water. He said that if the people would provide all their labour free of charge, he would give his services free to supervise the job. The cost would be £50,000.

"So where do you think our village can find that kind of money?" said John.

"You could always try the Danish Embassy," said Jansson.

Together they drew up a request for aid and a fortnight later came the good news that the money had been given. Then began weeks of work with gangs of men and women working with hoes and buckets. They cleared the silt and Jansson dismantled the old system and supervised the whole operation. Everything was completed by the end of the dry season of 1990. The dam began to fill during the 90/91 rains, and by January this year there was enough water in the dam to start irrigation in March. First the land below the dam would have to be cleared of grass and trees which had grown over the plots during the previous years of neglect. John Zumbwa said that my arrival was most opportune because he would be able to take me down to turn the taps to see how the first water would flow.

We set off with John carrying a sack over his shoulders containing the spanners and turning wheels. Daniel tapping the path with his stick followed along behind. We waded through the tall green grass that had overgrown the concrete channel where the large pipe ran. Two smaller taps had to be turned on first, then lower down there was the big stopcock. As soon as we had parted the grass, John knew that something was wrong. The dome of cast iron covering the valve was all askew on its setting. The six strong bolts which secured the flanges of the stopcock had been removed and it tilted drunkenly, held only by the central brass screw. A thief had come in the night and stolen them. But who? And why? This was vandalism of the worst kind. Who would want to sabotage something which was for the benefit of the whole village? Was this just mindless vandalism? or had it been done with some malicious intent. John was sick at heart and kept saying over and over again,

"Who has done this thing? How could they destroy all the work we have done? How can I face Jansson when I tell him what has happened?"

Daniel shuffled forward feeling the damage with his hands, his face almost touching the pipe as his glazed eyes peered close to the stopcock. He was quiet for a time and then he said,

"This has been done by a man who needs bolts to mend a plough or harrow or the broken shaft of an ox cart."

John agreed and tried to think of anyone he knew who had a spanner strong enough to have loosened the nuts and stolen the bolts. Fortunately the damage was not irreparable and as we walked back to the house we discussed the question of where to obtain replacements for the missing bolts. It would all take time but once Jansson got over the shock he would probably help again.

Tamed Guinea fowl are roosting in John's trees

We went to John's house and he introduced me to his wife Charity who is a teacher in the Chipapa school. She was squatting next to the fire in the round kitchen shelter, a simple structure of six upright poles supporting a low thatched roof. He showed me the little orchard which he had planted on the land which slopes down from the house to the lake. There were of course mangoes, guavas and pawpaws (papaya), but he had also grown bananas and a couple of pomegranate trees. He had planted a small area with kale but it had been swamped by a forest of wild amaranthus, which hardly mattered because this is more tasty and more nutritious than the best kale.

We sat on a couple of stools as he told me the story of the triumphs and failures of the last two years. As the sun went down and the light faded from the sky, the chickens came to roost in the tree. They had only recently been taught to do this by helping them to climb up the tree on long poles which sloped upwards from the ground propped against the lowest branches. They were much safer there than crowded into a chicken house where they fall easy prey to cerval cats and poisonous snakes. In another tree, John's little flock of tame guinea fowl had come to roost.

In my time at Chipapa we never saw guinea fowl in the villages because they do not seem to breed well in captivity. Now I find them everywhere, and John told me that by feeding them, a flock of cocks and hens can be sufficiently domesticated for the female birds to lay their eggs in nests on the ground in the bush round the house. Children go out to find the nests and bring eggs home to set under a broody hen. Not all the eggs are taken so the guinea fowl keep on laying, sometimes 90 to 100 eggs in one season. Guinea fowl are a much better proposition than chickens because they forage for their own food in the bush, seem to suffer from no diseases, and a full-grown bird fetches a high price in the urban market where the dark flesh is highly prized for its sweet tenderness.

Six of John's precious cattle had been stolen and four had died from 'black-leg disease' but still he had managed to plough, and he had proved to his own satisfaction that a green crop of sunn hemp ploughed into the soil was just as good, if not better, than growing the maize with an under-dressing of Compound D chemical fertilizer. He had also dug a well which went down thirty feet and had been lined with bricks, but as yet he had not money enough to buy a pump to use for the irrigation of his orchard and vegetable garden.

Over the years most of the things had been stolen from my house, but somewhere a bed was found for me and was made up in the little room which we had built for my son Robin when he came to spend a few months with me in 1969 before he went to university. He is now remembered by the villagers as the young man who made a little garden on the hillside by digging trenches with hoe and pickaxe in the soft rock. He filled the trenches with compost and cattle dung producing tomatoes which cropped heavily for six months.

It took me a while to get to sleep because the rain had enticed a thousand frogs to come out of the mud on the margin of the lake to mate and fill the night with raucous song. A family of rats chased one another up and down the sloping rafters of the roof, and from a mile away on the other side of the lake at the foot of the Mpande Hills came the urgent beat of drums. The people of Mwando's village must have brewed a lot of beer, for they danced and sang all through the night and the drums were still beating when I woke at six the next morning.

February 9th 1992 The Church on the hill

Sarah brought me a bowl of warm water to wash in, then made me a cup of 'tea' from masamba leaves. Sarah's household is too poor to afford to buy tea leaves but the masamba bush grows wild on the hillside; its leaves when dry are steeped in boiling water to make a liquid which looks very much like tea though tinged with red. I found I enjoyed it better than tea and wished I could take some home with me. There was no sugar nor milk so I had to eat the bowl of thin maize meal porridge as best I could.

A young man called Tele came to see me, so we sat on the veranda to talk. He is the agricultural extension officer in charge of the Chipapa Agricultural Camp, which is one of three 'camps' in the Kafue 'block.' He told me his life story; how he had passed the grade twelve examination, gone to the Agricultural Training College at Mpika where he met some born again Christians who changed his life. I decided for his sake to preach on the text 'you cannot enter the kingdom of Heaven unless you be born again'. As we talked, some girls in robes of pale green with hems sweeping the floor as they walked, came to gather purple bougainvillea blossom which they put in a rusty fruit tin to take to the church. At nine o'clock I walked the half mile to the little white-washed church on the hill beyond the school. It was built in 1965 with help from the Methodist missionaries at Kafue Mission seventeen miles away, although it was the people themselves who made the bricks and burnt them in a kiln.

When I preached there in the sixties, the congregation was seldom more than a dozen souls. Today the church was full with more than eighty people sitting on the wooden benches made by the village carpenter. There was a choir of twenty seven young men and women, all but one in white collared pale green gowns. The conductor, a youth of seventeen was distinguished by the black collar of his gown. And how they sang! What rhythmical movement of their bodies and their hands! During one song all but the three drummers moved out of the choir stall and danced in the aisle. Some of the old women got up to join them while some of the old men scowled disapproval from their seats (they had been brought up by the missionaries to believe that dancing in church was not a good thing.) With all the praying and preaching, the singing and reading in three languages, the service went on for two hours. Then there was another two hours of the annual church meeting when officers were elected: chairman, deputy chairman, secretary and treasurer, not only of

115

the church council but of the choir, the women's group, the stewards, the discipline committee etc. etc. Never have I seen democratic elections conducted with such meticulous attention to detail. Each person nominated for office had to be proposed and seconded, there had to be no less then three nominated who were then sent out to wait under the trees while votes were taken, numbers carefully recorded and the successful candidate recalled and congratulated. I am sure that the orderly manner in which Zambia conducted the democratic election of its new President owes much to the example set by the churches.

I spent the evening with John Zumbwa and Gilbert Shachikwa, the son of one of the four men who built the church here. Gilbert is about thirty years old, big boned and tall with a most engaging grin. He was elected today as chairman of the church discipline committee. I do not know what penance he demands from members for their misdemeanours but I guess he meters out the punishment with a twinkle in his eye. He and his brother are now working the land which was first allocated to their father when farm boundaries were demarcated at the time of resettlement in the 1940's.

These two men explained to me their ideas for Chipapa's long- term development. The re-establishment of irrigation below the dam will benefit perhaps fifty families. But the population is growing- and if young men and women are to be encouraged to see farming as a way of life they will need to have part of their farm irrigated, even if it is only a small plot for growing their fruit trees and vegetables and for making their fish ponds. There is underground water if wells and bore holes can be sunk. A request has been put to the Zambia Electricity Supply Corporation for an extension of the power line from the railway to Chipapa school and farms (see map). The bringing of electricity into this area for pumps and grinding mills opens up

116

all kinds of development possibilities. If only the World Bank would invest its money in Chipapa's farms rather than in Guy Scott's privatized tobacco estates!

For me this has been a high point in my journey because I see the new green shoots springing out of the wasteland of our past failures. Many of our concepts were right but we had only old men and women to work with, all the young men and girls had gone off to look for work in the towns. These old people, still held in the grip of tradition, may have had the will to break with the past but they had neither the education nor the competence to handle the problems of urban marketing and motorised passenger transport.

It was this competent management of simple things that was so lacking in the past and it is our hope that John Zumbwa will provide this in the future, for he is not only a well trained agriculturalist but has worked as an administrative officer at the Mount Makulu Agricultural Research Station.

After my return in 1992 we sent parcels of good second hand clothing to John and Charity Zumbwa which they promised to sell using the money to fund the various projects which the Young Farmers' Club had started. but we did not hear whether the parcels were arriving safely. Then Charity wrote to say that her husband was very unwell and although he went to see the doctors in the university teaching hospital in Lusaka the medicines they prescribed did not seem to do any good. At the end of the year we received a letter to say that he had been taken to a Salvation Army Mission hospital where he died.

I returned to Zambia in 1993 to visit projects in the Zambezi Valley and I called in at Chipapa on my way back. The entry in my diary for February 27th 1993 reads as follows:-

27th February 1993 Chipapa tragedy

This has been a sad and sorrowful day for me. I had somehow made myself believe that Charity, John's widow, would step into his shoes and keep things together until a new leader could be found. But I had forgotten what cruel things happen here when a man with property dies. In Tonga custom a man's wife is his property and in the past would have been inherited along with his children by a brother for whom she would become another wife.

When Charity married John Zumbwa ten years ago, he had two children of his own aged four and two, from his previous wife who died. Charity brought them up as her own and herself bore two, a boy and a girl. After John's death his relatives took everything from her including her two step children. All she kept were her clothes and blankets which she took, along with her own son and daughter when she fled to live with her widowed sister, in Matero, one of Lusaka's oldest and poorest suburbs. It has been a devastating experience especially for the two step-children who still regard Charity as their mother. Last week, the boy Norman ran away and somehow managed to find Charity in Matero. All he had taken for the twenty mile journey was a bottle of milk, and he arrived with nothing more than the clothes he stood up in.

I was taken to see what John had managed to do with his band of helpers before he died. They had built and burned a kiln of bricks, excavated two thirty yard long fish tanks, and prepared the fields for planting. All the time John had been feeling very unwell, but none of the doctors he consulted were able to tell him what was wrong. A week before he died, the Salvation Army doctors at Chikankata found a tumour in the bowel but it was too late to operate. Had it been diagnosed earlier he would still be with us. What a tragedy, what waste! He is indeed irreplaceable.

John's right-hand man is Obert aged 25 with nine years education but with a minimal understanding of English. As well as working on the development project he spends a couple of days a week going round the village as an agent of the Planned Parenthood Association. He is supposed to give talks on health education and AIDS, but I think that means not much more than distributing condoms. He had been promised some 'allowances' for this service but so far has not received anything. Everyone says he is a hard worker and they want him to be their new leader.

It is twenty five years since I first set foot in Chipapa, and on the surface so little seems to have changed. In spite of the good rains many of the fields have not been cultivated and those that have show little sign of yielding much of a crop. But there is more water in the dam than there has been for 20 years. New bolts have been found to mend the broken stop-cock and irrigated garden land which has lain fallow for three years can be revived when the dry season comes, so there is still hope.

I visited Zambia again in the wet season of 1995/6 and paid a brief visit to Chipapa. The following is an extract from my report:-

Report of Visit in 1996 - 7

The rains have been good and the men of the Farmers' Club proudly showed me their crops of tall maize which they had grown with help from the manure in their cattle kraals without the use of hybrid seed and chemical fertilizers. As I walked along the recently graded gravel road which runs from the school to the railway crossing, I met two young women each carrying a heavy sack of green french beans on their heads. They were taking them to Chilanga to catch the bus which would carry them early the next morning to the open market in Lusaka. They told me that the irrigated land below the dam had been extended and that there were over a hundred people growing vegetables for sale.

My mind went back thirty years to the time when I first went to live in the village when only one old man had a garden there. Then I had an image of the spirits of old Goodfellow the District Commissioner who first built the dam and John Zumbwa who got it repaired and I felt sure I could hear them rejoicing from their graves.

I heard the clatter of a diesel driven maize mill which I was told is owned and operated by the daughters of the women who used to run the poultry club. I found Obert watering his father's cattle at the lake side. They all looked to be in prime condition, from the suckling calves to the old cross bred Afrikander bull. He showed me his farm which he is in the process of taking over from his old father and pointed out the place where he has dug a well. He told me that he plans to put a hand pump on it from which he will irrigate a small garden which will be used to teach village girls who want to grow vegetables but have no chance of getting land below the dam.

In the late afternoon we gathered on the verandah of my old house, in the shade of the bougainvillea. I caught up with the village news and explained how I had come to Zambia this time to assist the Copperbelt women of ASAWA, (The Association for the Advancement of Women in Africa) to start to grow their own food using organic methods. I missed Daniel but then Sarah and her granddaughter Fanny (Janala's eldest daughter) carried him out of his house to greet me. He is now almost totally deaf and blind, trembling and shaking like a man with advanced Parkinson's Disease. I have no proof but I am of the opinion that he was suffering from the final effects of poisoned food which he ate when he went to pray at the bedside of Zunda the dying worker on the flower farm. Daniel hardly knew me but through his almost incoherent mumbling speech I heard him say that he knew he had not long to live and prayed to be allowed to die. Sarah had cared for Daniel through all the years of misery and she alone with a little help from Fanny has had to grow and prepare and cook every morsel of food he has eaten. In their desperate poverty they have nursed him and with her quiet courage and innate dignity Sarah has shown the triumph of the human spirit over all adversity.

POSTSCRIPT

In the middle of 1996 Daniel died and was buried in the village the same day. After the funeral, according to the custom of the people, his relatives like a flock of starving vultures descended on his home and took everything away, his plough, his harrow, his bed, his table and chair. One of them settled into the shell of his house and Sarah was chased away with nothing but her blanket and the clothes she stood up in to go and live with Janala on the Copperbelt. Two months later her son Chipo who had been living in my old house also died, probably from Aids, though no-one speaks openly about his cause of death.

However not all the news from Chipapa has been bad news. I was able to get £1000 from the Methodist Relief and Development Fund to send to Obert who has ordered a hand pump for his well and hopes to get the girls' gardening club started after the 1997 rains finish.

There is good news too from other parts of Zambia. On the Copperbelt ASAWA goes from strength to strength with more and more women being given basic training in organic food production. In the Zambezi Valley the Sustainable Agriculture and Tree Planting Programme is developing well under the competent leadership of Bazak Luungu, while on the plateau Ennias Michello is spreading the message of organic farming into all corners of the Southern Province. He proudly boasts that there is hardly a chief or chief's counsellor or village headman who has not received instruction in the use of natural fertilizers and the making of compost and the value of planting trees.

CONCLUSION

When Kaunda's government in 1964 had to chose a name for the new unit of currency at Independence they called it 'Kwacha', the English word for 'dawn'. For all of us in Zambia at that time it signified our political and economic hopes and aspirations for the future of our country. The currency was valued at two kwacha to the pound; today the value is two thousand kwacha to the pound. In 1964 Zambia's economy was booming; today the country is crippled by debt, and heavily dependent on massive injections of foreign aid.

What of the future?

The World Bank estimates that over 70% of Zambians live in severe poverty in a country so rich in natural resources of land, water, sunshine and trees that no man, woman or child need ever go hungry, nor lack anything needed for a full, free and happy life. While the economists, sociologists, moralists and politicians argue about the causes of poverty and suggest possible ways of eradicating it, there are signs that the people themselves are finding solutions.

Everywhere they are seeing the possibilities of changing their own destinies by changing their relationship with the land.

Even more significantly the government has admitted publicly for the first time that their policies for the land have failed. In March the Minister of Agriculture stated,

"The Input Recovery Fund meant for fertilizer purchases has collapsed because of loan defaults by farmers, credit coordinators and credit managers. The agricultural industry is in dire straights and needs to be seriously examined. Fertilizer imported from South Africa was delayed because of late payment for 1995 imports, and about 660,000 peasant farmers will go without. I've urged them to use manure".

Can anyone doubt that Zambia is ripe for an organic revolution?

MERFYN TEMPLE
CURRICULUM VITAE

1919

Second son of Methodist missionary parents in South China.

EDUCATION

Earnseat School, Arnside.
Leys School, Cambridge.
Richmond Theological College London School of Oriental and African Studies London.

1943

Appointed by Methodist Church to Northern Rhodesia.
Stationed at Broken Hill, Kafue, Mumbwa.

1948

Principal Nambala Rural Training Centre.

1957

General Secretary United Society for Christian Literature in Northern Rhodesia.

1958

President Christian Council of Northern Rhodesia.
Chairman Governors Mindolo Ecumenical Foundation.

1959

Member of Kenneth Kaunda's United National Independence Party: UNIP candidate Luanshya and Barotseland.

1963

Deputy Director Zambia Youth Service.

1965

Secretary Land Resettlement Board.

1967

Acting Commissioner Land Settlement.

1972

Lecturer National Institute Public Administration Lusaka National Administrator Ward and Village Development committees.

1974

Returned to Britain.

1976

Methodist Minister Wantage and Abingdon Circuit.

1977

Member of official delegation to Republic of China with SACU (Society for Anglo Chinese Understanding).

1984

Retired. Organic grower Upper Basildon.

1989

Cycle journey Nairobi to Kariba.
Subsequent visits to Zambia 1992, '93, '95, '96.

1992

Visit to Uganda with Kulika Trust previous to the setting up of Warren Farm Organic Agricultural Training Centre.
Member of Methodist Relief and Development Fund A.W.A.P (Africa Water and Agroforestry Programme).

Note

Copies of 'Elephants and Millipedes' and 'New Hope For Africa' may be obtained from:

Millipede Books
40 Thames Avenue
Pangbourne
Berkshire
RG8 7BY
Tel: 0118 984 5304

price £4.99 + £1.50 p&p